ANNE SEXTON (born Anne Gray Harvey; November 9, 1928 – October 4, 1974) was an American poet known for her highly personal, confessional verse. She won the Pulitzer Prize for poetry in 1967 for her book Live or Die. Her poetry details her long battle with depression, suicidal tendencies, and intimate details from her private life, including relationships with her husband and children, whom it was later alleged she physically and sexually assaulted..

Anne sexton

100 SELECTED POEMS

DELHI OPEN BOOKS

100 SELECTED POEMS
BY ANNE SEXTON

Published by

Delhi Open Books

G/F, 4771/23, Bharat Ram Road, Daryaganj, New Delhi-110002
Ph.: 91-11-42408081
E-mail: delhiopenbooks2016@gmail.com

ISBN: 978-93-94109-75-9

Cover, Typesetting, and Book Design by ROHIT

Printed & bound in India

Contents

45 Mercy Street

In my dream,
drilling into the marrow
of my entire bone,
my real dream,
I'm walking up and down Beacon Hill
searching for a street sign -
namely MERCY STREET.
Not there.
I try the Back Bay.
Not there.
Not there.
And yet I know the number.
45 Mercy Street.
I know the stained-glass window
of the foyer,
the three flights of the house
with its parquet floors.
I know the furniture and
mother, grandmother, great-grandmother,
the servants.
I know the cupboard of Spode
the boat of ice, solid silver,
where the butter sits in neat squares
like strange giant's teeth
on the big mahogany table.
I know it well.
Not there.
Where did you go?
45 Mercy Street,
with great-grandmother
kneeling in her whale-bone corset

and praying gently but fiercely
to the wash basin,
at five A.M.
at noon
dozing in her wiggy rocker,
grandfather taking a nap in the pantry,
grandmother pushing the bell for the downstairs maid,
and Nana rocking Mother with an oversized flower
on her forehead to cover the curl
of when she was good and when she was...
And where she was begat
and in a generation
the third she will beget,
me,
with the stranger's seed blooming
into the flower called Horrid.
I walk in a yellow dress
and a white pocketbook stuffed with cigarettes,
enough pills, my wallet, my keys,
and being twenty-eight, or is it forty-five?
I walk. I walk.
I hold matches at street signs
for it is dark,
as dark as the leathery dead
and I have lost my green Ford,
my house in the suburbs,
two little kids
sucked up like pollen by the bee in me
and a husband
who has wiped off his eyes
in order not to see my inside out
and I am walking and looking
and this is no dream
just my oily life
where the people are alibis

and the street is unfindable for an
entire lifetime.
Pull the shades down -
I don't care!
Bolt the door, mercy,
erase the number,
rip down the street sign,
what can it matter,
what can it matter to this cheapskate
who wants to own the past
that went out on a dead ship
and left me only with paper?
Not there.
I open my pocketbook,
as women do,
and fish swim back and forth
between the dollars and the lipstick.
I pick them out,
one by one
and throw them at the street signs,
and shoot my pocketbook
into the Charles River.
Next I pull the dream off
and slam into the cement wall
of the clumsy calendar
I live in,
my life,
and its hauled up
notebooks.

A Curse Against Elegies

Oh, love, why do we argue like this?
I am tired of all your pious talk.
Also, I am tired of all the dead.
They refuse to listen,
so leave them alone.
Take your foot out of the graveyard,
they are busy being dead.
Everyone was always to blame:
the last empty fifth of booze,
the rusty nails and chicken feathers
that stuck in the mud on the back doorstep,
the worms that lived under the cat's ear
and the thin-lipped preacher
who refused to call
except once on a flea-ridden day
when he came scuffing in through the yard
looking for a scapegoat.
I hid in the kitchen under the ragbag.
I refuse to remember the dead.
And the dead are bored with the whole thing.
But you - you go ahead,
go on, go on back down
into the graveyard,
lie down where you think their faces are;
talk back to your old bad dreams.

A Story For Rose On The Midnight Flight To Boston

Until tonight they were separate specialties,
different stories, the best of their own worst.
Riding my warm cabin home, I remember Betsy's
laughter; she laughed as you did, Rose, at the first
story. Someday, I promised her, I'll be someone
going somewhere and we plotted it in the humdrum
school for proper girls. The next April the plane
bucked me like a horse, my elevators turned
and fear blew down my throat, that last profane
gauge of a stomach coming up. And then returned
to land, as unlovely as any seasick sailor,
sincerely eighteen; my first story, my funny failure.
Maybe Rose, there is always another story,
better unsaid, grim or flat or predatory.
Half a mile down the lights of the in-between cities
turn up their eyes at me. And I remember Betsy's
story, the April night of the civilian air crash
and her sudden name misspelled in the evening paper,
the interior of shock and the paper gone in the trash
ten years now. She used the return ticket I gave her.
This was the rude kill of her; two planes cracking
in mid-air over Washington, like blind birds.
And the picking up afterwards, the morticians tracking
bodies in the Potomac and piecing them like boards
to make a leg or a face. There is only her miniature
photograph left, too long now for fear to remember.
Special tonight because I made her into a story
that I grew to know and savor.
A reason to worry,
Rose, when you fix an old death like that,
and outliving the impact, to find you've pretended.

We bank over Boston. I am safe. I put on my hat.
I am almost someone going home. The story has ended.

Admonitions To A Special Person

Watch out for power,
for its avalanche can bury you,
snow, snow, snow, smothering your mountain.
Watch out for hate,
it can open its mouth and you'll fling yourself out
to eat off your leg, an instant leper.
Watch out for friends,
because when you betray them,
as you will,
they will bury their heads in the toilet
and flush themselves away.
Watch out for intellect,
because it knows so much it knows nothing
and leaves you hanging upside down,
mouthing knowledge as your heart
falls out of your mouth.
Watch out for games, the actor's part,
the speech planned, known, given,
for they will give you away
and you will stand like a naked little boy,
pissing on your own child-bed.
Watch out for love
(unless it is true,
and every part of you says yes including the toes) ,
it will wrap you up like a mummy,
and your scream won't be heard
and none of your running will end.
Love? Be it man. Be it woman.
It must be a wave you want to glide in on,
give your body to it, give your laugh to it,
give, when the gravelly sand takes you,
your tears to the land. To love another is something
like prayer and can't be planned, you just fall

into its arms because your belief undoes your disbelief.
Special person,
if I were you I'd pay no attention
to admonitions from me,
made somewhat out of your words
and somewhat out of mine.
A collaboration.
I do not believe a word I have said,
except some, except I think of you like a young tree
with pasted-on leaves and know you'll root
and the real green thing will come.
Let go. Let go.
Oh special person,
possible leaves,
this typewriter likes you on the way to them,
but wants to break crystal glasses
in celebration,
for you,
when the dark crust is thrown off
and you float all around
like a happened balloon.

After Auschwitz

Anger,
as black as a hook,
overtakes me.
Each day,
each Nazi
took, at 8: 00 A.M., a baby
and sauteed him for breakfast
in his frying pan.
And death looks on with a casual eye
and picks at the dirt under his fingernail.
Man is evil,
I say aloud.
Man is a flower
that should be burnt,
I say aloud.
Man
is a bird full of mud,
I say aloud.
And death looks on with a casual eye
and scratches his anus.
Man with his small pink toes,
with his miraculous fingers
is not a temple
but an outhouse,
I say aloud.
Let man never again raise his teacup.
Let man never again write a book.
Let man never again put on his shoe.
Let man never again raise his eyes,
on a soft July night.
Never. Never. Never. Never. Never.

I say those things aloud.
I beg the Lord not to hear.

Again And Again And Again

You said the anger would come back
just as the love did.
I have a black look I do not
like. It is a mask I try on.
I migrate toward it and its frog
sits on my lips and defecates.
It is old. It is also a pauper.
I have tried to keep it on a diet.
I give it no unction.
There is a good look that I wear
like a blood clot. I have
sewn it over my left breast.
I have made a vocation of it.
Lust has taken plant in it
and I have placed you and your
child at its milk tip.
Oh the blackness is murderous
and the milk tip is brimming
and each machine is working
and I will kiss you when
I cut up one dozen new men
and you will die somewhat,
again and again.

All My Pretty Ones

Father, this year's jinx rides us apart
where you followed our mother to her cold slumber;
a second shock boiling its stone to your heart,
leaving me here to shuffle and disencumber
you from the residence you could not afford:
a gold key, your half of a woolen mill,
twenty suits from Dunne's, an English Ford,
the love and legal verbiage of another will,
boxes of pictures of people I do not know.
I touch their cardboard faces. They must go.
But the eyes, as thick as wood in this album,
hold me. I stop here, where a small boy
waits in a ruffled dress for someone to come…
for this soldier who holds his bugle like a toy
or for this velvet lady who cannot smile.
Is this your father's father, this Commodore
in a mailman suit? My father, time meanwhile
has made it unimportant who you are looking for.
I'll never know what these faces are all about.
I lock them into their book and throw them out.
This is the yellow scrapbook that you began
the year I was born; as crackling now and wrinkly
as tobacco leaves: clippings where Hoover outran
the Democrats, wiggling his dry finger at me
and Prohibition; news where the Hindenburg went
down and recent years where you went flush
on war. This year, solvent but sick, you meant
to marry that pretty widow in a one-month rush.
But before you had that second chance, I cried
on your fat shoulder. Three days later you died.
These are the snapshots of marriage, stopped in places.
Side by side at the rail toward Nassau now;

here, with the winner's cup at the speedboat races,
here, in tails at the Cotillion, you take a bow,
here, by our kennel of dogs with their pink eyes,
running like show-bred pigs in their chain-link pen;
here, at the horseshow where my sister wins a prize;
Now I fold you down, my drunkard, my navigator,
my first lost keeper, to love or look at later.
I hold a five-year diary that my mother kept
for three years, telling all she does not say
of your alcoholic tendency. You overslept,
she writes. My God, father, each Christmas Day
with your blood, will I drink down your glass
of wine? The diary of your hurly-burly years
goes to my shelf to wait for my age to pass.
Only in this hoarded span will love persevere.
Whether you are pretty or not, I outlive you,
bend down my strange face to yours and forgive you.

An Obsessive Combination Of Onotological Inscape,

Trickery And Love
Busy, with an idea for a code, I write
signals hurrying from left to right,
or right to left, by obscure routes,
for my own reasons; taking a word like writes
down tiers of tries until its secret rites
make sense; or until, suddenly, RATS
can amazingly and funnily become STAR
and right to left that small star
is mine, for my own liking, to stare
its five lucky pins inside out, to store
forever kindly, as if it were a star
I touched and a miracle I really wrote.

And One For My Dame

A born salesman,
my father made all his dough
by selling wool to Fieldcrest, Woolrich and Faribo.
A born talker,
he could sell one hundred wet-down bales
of that white stuff. He could clock the miles and the sales
and make it pay.
At home each sentence he would utter
had first pleased the buyer who'd paid him off in butter.
Each word
had been tried over and over, at any rate,
on the man who was sold by the man who filled my plate.
My father hovered
over the Yorkshire pudding and the beef:
a peddler, a hawker, a merchant and an Indian chief.
Roosevelt! Willkie! and war!
How suddenly gauche I was
with my old-maid heart and my funny teenage applause.
Each night at home
my father was in love with maps
while the radio fought its battles with Nazis and Japs.
Except when he hid
in his bedroom on a three-day drunk,
he typed out complex itineraries, packed his trunk,
his matched luggage
and pocketed a confirmed reservation,
his heart already pushing over the
red routes of the nation.
I sit at my desk
each night with no place to go,
opening thee wrinkled maps of Milwaukee and Buffalo,
the whole U.S.,

its cemeteries, its arbitrary time zones,
through routes like small veins, capitals like small stones.
He died on the road,
his heart pushed from neck to back,
his white hanky signaling from the window of the Cadillac.
My husband,
as blue-eyed as a picture book, sells wool:
boxes of card waste, laps and rovings he can pull
to the thread
and say Leicester, Rambouillet, Merino,
a half-blood, it's greasy and thick, yellow as old snow.
And when you drive off, my darling,
Yes, sir! Yes, sir! It's one for my dame,
your sample cases branded with my father's name,
your itinerary open,
its tolls ticking and greedy,
its highways built up like new loves, raw and speedy.

Angels Of The Love Affair

'Angels of the love affair, do you know that other,
the dark one, that other me? '
1. ANGEL OF FIRE AND GENITALS
Angel of fire and genitals, do you know slime,
that green mama who first forced me to sing,
who put me first in the latrine, that pantomime
of brown where I was beggar and she was king?
I said, 'The devil is down that festering hole.'
Then he bit me in the buttocks and took over my soul.
Fire woman, you of the ancient flame, you
of the Bunsen burner, you of the candle,
you of the blast furnace, you of the barbecue,
you of the fierce solar energy, Mademoiselle,
take some ice, take some snow, take a month of rain
and you would gutter in the dark, cracking up your brain.
Mother of fire, let me stand at your devouring gate
as the sun dies in your arms and you loosen it's terrible weight.
2. ANGEL OF CLEAN SHEETS
Angel of clean sheets, do you know bedbugs?
Once in the madhouse they came like specks of cinnamon
as I lay in a choral cave of drugs,
as old as a dog, as quiet as a skeleton.
Little bits of dried blood. One hundred marks
upon the sheet. One hundred kisses in the dark.
White sheets smelling of soap and Clorox
have nothing to do with this night of soil,
nothing to do with barred windows and multiple locks
and all the webbing in the bed, the ultimate recoil.
I have slept in silk and in red and in black.
I have slept on sand and, on fall night, a haystack.
I have known a crib. I have known the tuck-in of a child
but inside my hair waits the night I was defiled.

3. ANGEL OF FLIGHT AND SLEIGH BELLS

Angel of flight and sleigh bells, do you know paralysis,
that ether house where your arms and legs are cement?
You are as still as a yardstick. You have a doll's kiss.
The brain whirls in a fit. The brain is not evident.
I have gone to that same place without a germ or a stroke.
A little solo act-that lady with the brain that broke.
In this fashion I have become a tree.
I have become a vase you can pick up or drop at will,
inanimate at last. What unusual luck! My body
passively resisting. Part of the leftovers. Part of the kill.
Angels of flight, you soarer, you flapper, you floater,
you gull that grows out of my back in the drreams I prefer,
stay near. But give me the totem. Give me the shut eye
where I stand in stone shoes as the world's bicycle goes by.

4. ANGEL OF HOPE AND CALENDARS

Angel of hope and calendars, do you know despair?
That hole I crawl into with a box of Kleenex,
that hole where the fire woman is tied to her chair,
that hole where leather men are wringing their necks,
where the sea has turned into a pond of urine.
There is no place to wash and no marine beings to stir in.
In this hole your mother is crying out each day.
Your father is eating cake and digging her grave.
In this hole your baby is strangling. Your mouth is clay.
Your eyes are made of glass. They break. You are not brave.
You are alone like a dog in a kennel. Your hands
break out in boils. Your arms are cut and bound by bands
of wire. Your voice is out there. Your voice is strange.
There are no prayers here. Here there
is no change.

5. ANGEL OF BLIZZARDS AND BLACKOUTS

Angle of blizzards and blackouts, do you know raspberries,
those rubies that sat in the tree of my grandfather's garden?
You of the snow tires, you of the sugary wings, you freeze
me out. Let me crawl through the patch. Let me be ten.
Let me pick those sweet kisses, thief that I was,
as the sea on my left slapped its applause.
Only my grandfather was allowed there. Or the maid
who came with a scullery pan to pick for breakfast.
She of the rolls that floated in the air, she of the inlaid
woodwork all greasy with lemon, she of the feather and dust,
not I. Nonetheless I came sneaking across the salt lawn
in bare feet and jumping-jack pajamas in the spongy dawn.
Oh Angel of the blizzard and blackout, Madam white face,
take me back to that red mouth, that July 21st place.

6. ANGEL OF BEACH HOUSES AND PICNICS

Angel of beach houses and picnics, do you know solitaire?
Fifty-two reds and blacks and only myself to blame.
My blood buzzes like a hornet's nest. I sit in a kitchen chair
at a table set for one. The silverware is the same
and the glass and the sugar bowl. I hear my lungs fill and expel
as in an operation. But I have no one left to tell.
Once I was a couple. I was my own king and queen
with cheese and bread and rosé on the rocks of Rockport.
Once I sunbathed in the buff, all brown and lean,
watching the toy sloops go by, holding court
for busloads of tourists. Once I called breakfast the sexiest
meal of the day. Once I invited arrest
at the peace march in Washington.
Once I was young and bold
and left hundreds of unmatched people out in the cold.

Anna Who Was Mad

Anna who was mad,
I have a knife in my armpit.
When I stand on tiptoe I tap out messages.
Am I some sort of infection?
Did I make you go insane?
Did I make the sounds go sour?
Did I tell you to climb out the window?
Forgive. Forgive.
Say not I did.
Say not.
Say.
Speak Mary-words into our pillow.
Take me the gangling twelve-year-old
into your sunken lap.
Whisper like a buttercup.
Eat me. Eat me up like cream pudding.
Take me in.
Take me.
Take.
Give me a report on the condition of my soul.
Give me a complete statement of my actions.
Hand me a jack-in-the-pulpit and let me listen in.
Put me in the stirrups and bring a tour group through.
Number my sins on the grocery list and let me buy.
Did I make you go insane?
Did I turn up your earphone and let a siren
drive through?
Did I open the door for the mustached psychiatrist
who dragged you out like a gold cart?
Did I make you go insane?
From the grave write me, Anna!

You are nothing but ashes but nevertheless
pick up the Parker Pen I gave you.
Write me.
Write.

As It Was Written

Earth, earth,
riding your merry-go-round
toward extinction,
right to the roots,
thickening the oceans like gravy,
festering in your caves,
you are becoming a latrine.
Your trees are twisted chairs.
Your flowers moan at their mirrors,
and cry for a sun that doesn't wear a mask.
Your clouds wear white,
trying to become nuns
and say novenas to the sky.
The sky is yellow with its jaundice,
and its veins spill into the rivers
where the fish kneel down
to swallow hair and goat's eyes.
All in all, I'd say,
the world is strangling.
And I, in my bed each night,
listen to my twenty shoes
converse about it.
And the moon,
under its dark hood,
falls out of the sky each night,
with its hungry red mouth
to suck at my scars.

August 17th

Surely I will be disquieted
by the hospital, that body zonebodies
wrapped in elastic bands,
bodies cased in wood or used like telephones,
bodies crucified up onto their crutches,
bodies wearing rubber bags between their legs,
bodies vomiting up their juice like detergent, Here in this house
there are other bodies.
Whenever I see a six-year-old
swimming in our aqua pool
a voice inside me says what can't be told...
Ha, someday you'll be old and withered
and tubes will be in your nose
drinking up your dinner.
Someday you'll go backward. You'll close
up like a shoebox and you'll be cursed
as you push into death feet first.
Here in the hospital, I say,
that is not my body, not my body.
I am not here for the doctors
to read like a recipe.
No. I am a daisy girl
blowing in the wind like a piece of sun.
On ward 7 there are daisies, all butter and pearl
but beside a blind man who can only
eat up the petals and count to ten.
The nurses skip rope around him and shiver
as his eyes wiggle like mercury and then
they dance from patient to patient to patient
throwing up little paper medicine cups and playing
catch with vials of dope as they wait for new accidents.

Bodies made of synthetics. Bodies swaddled like dolls
whom I visit and cajole and all they do is hum
like computers doing up our taxes, dollar by dollar.
Each body is in its bunker. The surgeon applies his gum.
Each body is fitted quickly into its ice-cream pack
and then stitched up again for the long voyage
back.

August 8th

Listen here. I've never played it safe
in spite of what the critics say.
Ask my imaginary brother, that waif,
that childhood best friend who comes to play
dress-up and stick-up and jacks and Pick-Up-Sticks,
bike downtown, stick out tongues at the Catholics.
Or form a Piss Club where we all go
in the bushes and peek at each other's sex.
Pop-gunning the street lights like crows.
Not knowing what to do with funny Kotex
so wearing it in our school shoes. Friend, friend,
spooking my lonely hours you were there, but pretend.

Baby Picture

It's in the heart of the grape
where that smile lies.
It's in the good-bye-bow in the hair
where that smile lies.
It's in the clerical collar of the dress
where that smile lies.
What smile?
The smile of my seventh year,
caught here in the painted photograph.
It's peeling now, age has got it,
a kind of cancer of the background
and also in the assorted features.
It's like a rotten flag
or a vegetable from the refrigerator,
pocked with mold.
I am aging without sound,
into darkness, darkness.
Anne,
who are you?
I open the vein
and my blood rings like roller skates.
I open the mouth
and my teeth are an angry army.
I open the eyes
and they go sick like dogs
with what they have seen.
I open the hair
and it falls apart like dust balls.
I open the dress
and I see a child bent on a toilet seat.
I crouch there, sitting dumbly
pushing the enemas out like ice cream,

letting the whole brown world
turn into sweets.
Anne,
who are you?
Merely a kid keeping alive.

Barefoot

Loving me with my shoes off
means loving my long brown legs,
sweet dears, as good as spoons;
and my feet, those two children
let out to play naked. Intricate nubs,
my toes. No longer bound.
And what's more, see toenails and
all ten stages, root by root.
All spirited and wild, this little
piggy went to market and this little piggy
stayed. Long brown legs and long brown toes.
Further up, my darling, the woman
is calling her secrets, little houses,
little tongues that tell you.
There is no one else but us
in this house on the land spit.
The sea wears a bell in its navel.
And I'm your barefoot wench for a
whole week. Do you care for salami?
No. You'd rather not have a scotch?
No. You don't really drink. You do
drink me. The gulls kill fish,
crying out like three-year-olds.
The surf's a narcotic, calling out,
I am, I am, I am
all night long. Barefoot,
I drum up and down your back.
In the morning I run from door to door
of the cabin playing chase me.
Now you grab me by the ankles.
Now you work your way up the legs
and come to pierce me at my hunger mark

Bat

His awful skin
stretched out by some tradesman
is like my skin, here between my fingers,
a kind of webbing, a kind of frog.
Surely when first born my face was this tiny
and before I was born surely I could fly.
Not well, mind you, only a veil of skin
from my arms to my waist.
I flew at night, too. Not to be seen
for if I were I'd be taken down.
In August perhaps as the trees rose to the stars
I have flown from leaf to leaf in the thick dark.
If you had caught me with your flashlight
you would have seen a pink corpse with wings,
out, out, from her mother's belly, all furry
and hoarse skimming over the houses, the armies.
That's why the dogs of your house sniff me.
They know I'm something to be caught
somewhere in the cemetery hanging upside down
like a misshapen udder.

Briar Rose (Sleeping Beauty)

Consider
a girl who keeps slipping off,
arms limp as old carrots,
into the hypnotist's trance,
into a spirit world
speaking with the gift of tongues.
She is stuck in the time machine,
suddenly two years old sucking her thumb,
as inward as a snail,
learning to talk again.
She's on a voyage.
She is swimming further and further back,
up like a salmon,
struggling into her mother's pocketbook.
Little doll child,
come here to Papa.
Sit on my knee.
I have kisses for the back of your neck.
A penny for your thoughts, Princess.
I will hunt them like an emerald.
Come be my snooky
and I will give you a root.
That kind of voyage,
rank as a honeysuckle.
Once
a king had a christening
for his daughter Briar Rose
and because he had only twelve gold plates
he asked only twelve fairies
to the grand event.
The thirteenth fairy,

her fingers as long and thing as straws,
her eyes burnt by cigarettes,
her uterus an empty teacup,
arrived with an evil gift.
She made this prophecy:
The princess shall prick herself
on a spinning wheel in her fifteenth year
and then fall down dead.
Kaputt!
The court fell silent.
The king looked like Munch's Scream
Fairies' prophecies,
in times like those,
held water.
However the twelfth fairy
had a certain kind of eraser
and thus she mitigated the curse
changing that death
into a hundred-year sleep.
The king ordered every spinning wheel
exterminated and exorcised.
Briar Rose grew to be a goddess
and each night the king
bit the hem of her gown
to keep her safe.
He fastened the moon up
with a safety pin
to give her perpetual light
He forced every male in the court
to scour his tongue with Bab-o
lest they poison the air she dwelt in.
Thus she dwelt in his odor.
Rank as honeysuckle.
On her fifteenth birthday
she pricked her finger

on a charred spinning wheel
and the clocks stopped.
Yes indeed. She went to sleep.
The king and queen went to sleep,
the courtiers, the flies on the wall.
The fire in the hearth grew still
and the roast meat stopped crackling.
The trees turned into metal
and the dog became china.
They all lay in a trance,
each a catatonic
stuck in a time machine.

Even the frogs were zombies.
Only a bunch of briar roses grew
forming a great wall of tacks
around the castle.
Many princes
tried to get through the brambles
for they had heard much of Briar Rose
but they had not scoured their tongues
so they were held by the thorns
and thus were crucified.
In due time
a hundred years passed
and a prince got through.
The briars parted as if for Moses
and the prince found the tableau intact.
He kissed Briar Rose
and she woke up crying:
Daddy! Daddy!
Presto! She's out of prison!
She married the prince
and all went well
except for the fear -

the fear of sleep.
Briar Rose
was an insomniac...
She could not nap
or lie in sleep
without the court chemist
mixing her some knock-out drops
and never in the prince's presence.
If if is to come, she said,
sleep must take me unawares
while I am laughing or dancing
so that I do not know that brutal place
where I lie down with cattle prods,
the hole in my cheek open.
Further, I must not dream
for when I do I see the table set
and a faltering crone at my place,
her eyes burnt by cigarettes
as she eats betrayal like a slice of meat.

I must not sleep
for while I'm asleep I'm ninety
and think I'm dying.
Death rattles in my throat
like a marble.
I wear tubes like earrings.
I lie as still as a bar of iron.
You can stick a needle
through my kneecap and I won't flinch.
I'm all shot up with Novocain.
This trance girl
is yours to do with.
You could lay her in a grave,
an awful package,
and shovel dirt on her face

and she'd never call back: Hello there!
But if you kissed her on the mouth
her eyes would spring open
and she'd call out: Daddy! Daddy!
Presto!
She's out of prison.
There was a theft.
That much I am told.
I was abandoned.
That much I know.
I was forced backward.
I was forced forward.
I was passed hand to hand
like a bowl of fruit.
Each night I am nailed into place
and forget who I am.
Daddy?
That's another kind of prison.
It's not the prince at all,
but my father
drunkeningly bends over my bed,
circling the abyss like a shark,
my father thick upon me
like some sleeping jellyfish.
What voyage is this, little girl?
This coming out of prison?
God help -
this life after death?

Buying The Whore

You are the roast beef I have purchased
and I stuff you with my very own onion.
You are a boat I have rented by the hour
and I steer you with my rage until you run aground.
You are a glass that I have paid to shatter
and I swallow the pieces down with my spit.
You are the grate I warm my trembling hands on,
searing the flesh until it's nice and juicy.
You stink like my Mama under your bra
and I vomit into your hand like a jackpot
its cold hard quarters.

Christmas Eve

Oh sharp diamond, my mother!
I could not count the cost
of all your faces, your moodsthat
present that I lost.
Sweet girl, my deathbed,
my jewel-fingered lady,
your portrait flickered all night
by the bulbs of the tree.
Your face as calm as the moon
over a mannered sea,
presided at the family reunion,
the twelve grandchildren
you used to wear on your wrist,
a three-months-old baby,
a fat check you never wrote,
the red-haired toddler who danced the twist,
your aging daughters, each one a wife,
each one talking to the family cook,
each one avoiding your portrait,
each one aping your life.
Later, after the party,
after the house went to bed,
I sat up drinking the Christmas brandy,
watching your picture,
letting the tree move in and out of focus.
The bulbs vibrated.
They were a halo over your forehead.
Then they were a beehive,
blue, yellow, green, red;
each with its own juice, each hot and alive
stinging your face. But you did not move.
I continued to watch, forcing myself,

waiting, inexhaustible, thirty-five.
I wanted your eyes, like the shadows
of two small birds, to change.
But they did not age.

The smile that gathered me in, all wit,
all charm, was invincible.
Hour after hour I looked at your face
but I could not pull the roots out of it.
Then I watched how the sun hit your red sweater, your withered
neck,
your badly painted flesh-pink skin.
You who led me by the nose, I saw you as you were.
Then I thought of your body
as one thinks of murder-
Then I said Mary-
Mary, Mary, forgive me
and then I touched a present for the child,
the last I bred before your death;
and then I touched my breast
and then I touched the floor
and then my breast again as if,
somehow, it were one of yours.

Cigarettes And Whiskey And Wild, Wild Women

(from a song)
Perhaps I was born kneeling,
born coughing on the long winter,
born expecting the kiss of mercy,
born with a passion for quickness
and yet, as things progressed,
I learned early about the stockade
or taken out, the fume of the enema.
By two or three I learned not to kneel,
not to expect, to plant my fires underground
where none but the dolls, perfect and awful,
could be whispered to or laid down to die.
Now that I have written many words,
and let out so many loves, for so many,
and been altogether what I always was—
a woman of excess, of zeal and greed,
I find the effort useless.
Do I not look in the mirror,
these days,
and see a drunken rat avert her eyes?
Do I not feel the hunger so acutely
that I would rather die than look
into its face?
I kneel once more,
in case mercy should come
in the nick of time.

Cinderella

You always read about it:
the plumber with the twelve children
who wins the Irish Sweepstakes.
From toilets to riches.
That story.
Or the nursemaid,
some luscious sweet from Denmark
who captures the oldest son's heart.
from diapers to Dior.
That story.
Or a milkman who serves the wealthy,
eggs, cream, butter, yogurt, milk,
the white truck like an ambulance
who goes into real estate
and makes a pile.
From homogenized to martinis at lunch.
Or the charwoman
who is on the bus when it cracks up
and collects enough from the insurance.
From mops to Bonwit Teller.
That story.
Once
the wife of a rich man was on her deathbed
and she said to her daughter Cinderella:
Be devout. Be good. Then I will smile
down from heaven in the seam of a cloud.
The man took another wife who had
two daughters, pretty enough
but with hearts like blackjacks.
Cinderella was their maid.
She slept on the sooty hearth each night
and walked around looking like Al Jolson.

Her father brought presents home from town,
jewels and gowns for the other women
but the twig of a tree for Cinderella.

She planted that twig on her mother's grave
and it grew to a tree where a white dove sat.
Whenever she wished for anything the dove
would dropp it like an egg upon the ground.
The bird is important, my dears, so heed him.
Next came the ball, as you all know.
It was a marriage market.
The prince was looking for a wife.
All but Cinderella were preparing
and gussying up for the event.
Cinderella begged to go too.
Her stepmother threw a dish of lentils
into the cinders and said: Pick them
up in an hour and you shall go.
The white dove brought all his friends;
all the warm wings of the fatherland came,
and picked up the lentils in a jiffy.
No, Cinderella, said the stepmother,
you have no clothes and cannot dance.
That's the way with stepmothers.
Cinderella went to the tree at the grave
and cried forth like a gospel singer:
Mama! Mama! My turtledove,
send me to the prince's ball!
The bird dropped down a golden dress
and delicate little slippers.
Rather a large package for a simple bird.
So she went. Which is no surprise.
Her stepmother and sisters didn't
recognize her without her cinder face
and the prince took her hand on the spot

and danced with no other the whole day.
As nightfall came she thought she'd better
get home. The prince walked her home
and she disappeared into the pigeon house
and although the prince took an axe and broke
it open she was gone. Back to her cinders.
These events repeated themselves for three days.
However on the third day the prince
covered the palace steps with cobbler's wax
and Cinderella's gold shoe stuck upon it.
Now he would find whom the shoe fit
and find his strange dancing girl for keeps.
He went to their house and the two sisters
were delighted because they had lovely feet.
The eldest went into a room to try the slipper on
but her big toe got in the way so she simply
sliced it off and put on the slipper.
The prince rode away with her until the white dove
told him to look at the blood pouring forth.
That is the way with amputations.
They just don't heal up like a wish.
The other sister cut off her heel
but the blood told as blood will.
The prince was getting tired.
He began to feel like a shoe salesman.
But he gave it one last try.
This time Cinderella fit into the shoe
like a love letter into its envelope.
At the wedding ceremony
the two sisters came to curry favor
and the white dove pecked their eyes out.
Two hollow spots were left
like soup spoons.
Cinderella and the prince
lived, they say, happily ever after,

like two dolls in a museum case
never bothered by diapers or dust,
never arguing over the timing of an egg,
never telling the same story twice,
never getting a middle-aged spread,
their darling smiles pasted on for eternity.
Regular Bobbsey Twins.
That story.

Clothes

Put on a clean shirt
before you die, some Russian said.
Nothing with drool, please,
no egg spots, no blood,
no sweat, no sperm.
You want me clean, God,
so I'll try to comply.
The hat I was married in,
will it do?
White, broad, fake flowers in a tiny array.
It's old-fashioned, as stylish as a bedbug,
but is suits to die in something nostalgic.
And I'll take
my painting shirt
washed over and over of course
spotted with every yellow kitchen I've painted.
God, you don't mind if I bring all my kitchens?
They hold the family laughter and the soup.
For a bra
(need we mention it?) ,
the padded black one that my lover demeaned
when I took it off.
He said, 'Where'd it all go? '
And I'll take
the maternity skirt of my ninth month,
a window for the love-belly
that let each baby pop out like and apple,
the water breaking in the restaurant,
making a noisy house I'd like to die in.
For underpants I'll pick white cotton,
the briefs of my childhood,

for it was my mother's dictum
that nice girls wore only white cotton.
If my mother had lived to see it

she would have put a WANTED sign up in the post office
for the black, the red, the blue I've worn.
Still, it would be perfectly fine with me
to die like a nice girl
smelling of Clorox and Duz.
Being sixteen-in-the-pants
I would die full of questions.

Cockroach

Roach, foulest of creatures,
who attacks with yellow teeth
and an army of cousins big as shoes,
you are lumps of coal that are mechanized
and when I turn on the light you scuttle
into the corners and there is this hiss upon the land.
Yet I know you are only the common angel
turned into, by way of enchantment, the ugliest.
Your uncle was made into an apple.
Your aunt was made into a Siamese cat,
all the rest were made into butterflies
but because you lied to God outrightlytold
him that all things on earth were in order-
He turned his wrath upon you and said,
I will make you the most loathsome,
I will make you into God's lie,
and never will a little girl fondle you
or hold your dark wings cupped in her palm.
But that was not true. Once in New Orleans
with a group of students a roach fled across
the floor and I shrieked and she picked it up
in her hands and held it from my fear for one hour.
And held it like a diamond ring that should not escape.
These days even the devil is getting overturned
and held up to the light like a glass of water.

Consorting With Angels

I was tired of being a woman,
tired of the spoons and the post,
tired of my mouth and my breasts,
tired of the cosmetics and the silks.
There were still men who sat at my table,
circled around the bowl I offered up.
The bowl was filled with purple grapes
and the flies hovered in for the scent
and even my father came with his white bone.
But I was tired of the gender things.
Last night I had a dream
and I said to it...
'You are the answer.
You will outlive my husband and my father.'
In that dream there was a city made of chains
where Joan was put to death in man's clothes
and the nature of the angels went unexplained,
no two made in the same species,
one with a nose, one with an ear in its hand,
one chewing a star and recording its orbit,
each one like a poem obeying itself,
performing God's functions,
a people apart.
'You are the answer, '
I said, and entered,
lying down on the gates of the city.
Then the chains were fastened around me
and I lost my common gender and my final aspect.
Adam was on the left of me
and Eve was on the right of me,
both thoroughly inconsistent with the world
of reason.

We wove our arms together
and rode under the sun.
I was not a woman anymore,
not one thing or the other.
O daughters of Jerusalem,

the king has brought me into his chamber.
I am black and I am beautiful.
I've been opened and undressed.
I have no arms or legs.
I'm all one skin like a fish.
I'm no more a woman
than Christ was a man.

Courage

It is in the small things we see it.
The child's first step,
as awesome as an earthquake.
The first time you rode a bike,
wallowing up the sidewalk.
The first spanking when your heart
went on a journey all alone.
When they called you crybaby
or poor or fatty or crazy
and made you into an alien,
you drank their acid
and concealed it.
Later,
if you faced the death of bombs and bullets
you did not do it with a banner,
you did it with only a hat to
comver your heart.
You did not fondle the weakness inside you
though it was there.
Your courage was a small coal
that you kept swallowing.
If your buddy saved you
and died himself in so doing,
then his courage was not courage,
it was love; love as simple as shaving soap.
Later,
if you have endured a great despair,
then you did it alone,
getting a transfusion from the fire,
picking the scabs off your heart,
then wringing it out like a sock.

Next, my kinsman, you powdered your sorrow,
you gave it a back rub
and then you covered it with a blanket
and after it had slept a while
it woke to the wings of the roses
and was transformed.
Later,
when you face old age and its natural conclusion
your courage will still be shown in the little ways,
each spring will be a sword you'll sharpen,
those you love will live in a fever of love,
and you'll bargain with the calendar
and at the last moment
when death opens the back door
you'll put on your carpet slippers
and stride out.

Cripples And Other Stories

My doctor, the comedian
I called you every time
and made you laugh yourself
when I wrote this silly rhyme...
Each time I give lectures
or gather in the grants
you send me off to boarding school
in training pants.
God damn it, father-doctor,
I'm really thirty-six.
I see dead rats in the toilet.
I'm one of the lunatics.
Disgusted, mother put me
on the potty. She was good at this.
My father was fat on scotch.
It leaked from every orifice.
Oh the enemas of childhood,
reeking of outhouses and shame!
Yet you rock me in your arms
and whisper my nickname.
Or else you hold my hand
and teach me love too late.
And that's the hand of the arm
they tried to amputate.
Though I was almost seven
I was an awful brat.
I put it in the Easy Wringer.
It came out nice and flat.
I was an instant cripple
from my finger to my shoulder.
The laundress wept and swooned.

My mother had to hold her.
I know I was a cripple.
Of course, I'd known it from the start.
My father took the crowbar
and broke the wringer's heart.
The surgeons shook their heads.
They really didn't know-
Would the cripple inside of me
be a cripple that would show?
My father was a perfect man,
clean and rich and fat.
My mother was a brilliant thing.
She was good at that.
You hold me in your arms.
How strange that you're so tender!
Child-woman that I am,
you think that you can mend her.
As for the arm,
unfortunately it grew.
Though mother said a withered arm
would put me in Who's Who.
For years she has described it.
She sang it like a hymn.
By then she loved the shrunken thing,
my little withered limb.
My father's cells clicked each night,
intent on making money.
And as for my cells, they brooded,
little queens, on honey.
Oh boys too, as a matter of fact,
and cigarettes and cars.
Mother frowned at my wasted life.
My father smoked cigars.

My cheeks blossomed with maggots.

I picked at them like pearls.
I covered them with pancake.
I wound my hair in curls.
My father didn't know me
but you kiss me in my fever.
My mother knew me twice
and then I had to leave her.
But those are just two stories
and I have more to tell
from the outhouse, the greenhouse
where you draw me out of hell.
Father, I am thirty-six,
yet I lie here in your crib.
I'm getting born again, Adam,
as you prod me with your rib.

Crossing The Atlantic

We sail out of season into on oyster-gray wind,
over a terrible hardness.
Where Dickens crossed with mal de mer
in twenty weeks or twenty days
I cross toward him in five.
Wraped in robesnot
like Caesar but like liver with bacon-
I rest on the stern
burning my mouth with a wind-hot ash,
watching my ship
bypass the swells
as easily as an old woman reads a palm.
I think; as I look North, that a field of mules
lay down to die.
The ship is 27 hours out.
I have entered her.
She might be a whale,
sleeping 2000 and ship's company,
the last 40¢ martini
and steel staterooms where night goes on forever.
Being inside them is, I think,
the way one would dig into a planet
and forget the word light.
I have walked cities,
miles of mole alleys with carpets.
Inside I have been ten girls who speak French.
They languish everywhere like bedsheets.
Oh my Atlantic of the cracked shores,
those blemished gates of Rockport and Boothbay,
those harbor smells like the innards of animals!
Old childish Queen, where did you go,

you bayer at wharfs and Victorian houses?
I have read each page of my mother's voyage.
I have read each page of her mother's voyage.
I have learned their words as they learned Dickens'.
I have swallowed these words like bullets.

But I have forgotten the last guest-terror.
Unlike them, I cannot toss in the cabin
as in childbirth.
Now always leaving me in the West
is the wake,
a ragged bridal veil, unexplained,
seductive, always rushing down the stairs,
never detained, never enough.
The ship goes on
as though nothing else were happening.
Generation after generation,
I go her way.
She will run East, knot by knot, over an old bloodstream,
stripping it clear,
each hour ripping it, pounding, pounding,
forcing through as through a virgin.
Oh she is so quick!
This dead street never stops!

‘Daddy’ Warbucks

What's missing is the eyeballs
in each of us, but it doesn't matter
because you've got the bucks, the bucks, the bucks.
You let me touch them, fondle the green faces
lick at their numbers and it lets you be
my ‘Daddy! ‘ ‘Daddy! ‘ and though I fought all alone
with molesters and crooks, I knew your money
would save me, your courage, your ‘I've had
considerable experience as a soldier...
fighting to win millions for myself, it's true.
But I did win, ‘ and me praying for ‘our men out there’
just made it okay to be an orphan whose blood was no one's,
whose curls were hung up on a wire machine and electrified,
while you built and unbuilt intrigues called nations,
and did in the bad ones, always, always,
and always came at my perils, the black Christs of childhood,
always came when my heart stood naked in the street
and they threw apples at it or twelve-day-old-dead-fish.
‘Daddy! ‘ ‘Daddy, ‘ we all won that war,
when you sang me the money songs
Annie, Annie you sang
and I knew you drove a pure gold car
and put diamonds in you coke
for the crunchy sound, the adorable sound
and the moon too was in your portfolio,
as well as the ocean with its sleepy dead.
And I was always brave, wasn't I?
I never bled?
I never saw a man expose himself.
No. No.
I never saw a drunkard in his blubber.

I never let lightning go in one car and out the other.
And all the men out there were never to come.
Never, like a deluge, to swim over my breasts
and lay their lamps in my insides.
No. No.
Just me and my 'Daddy'
and his tempestuous bucks
rolling in them like corn flakes
and only the bad ones died.
But I died yesterday,
'Daddy, ' I died,
swallowing the Nazi-Jap animal
and it won't get out
it keeps knocking at my eyes,
my big orphan eyes,
kicking! Until eyeballs pop out
and even my dog puts up his four feet
and lets go
of his military secret
with his big red tongue
flying up and down
like yours should have
as we board our velvet train.

Demon

A young man is afraid of his demon and puts his hand
over the demon's mouth sometimes...- D. H. Lawrence
I mentioned my demon to a friend
and the friend swam in oil and came forth to me
greasy and cryptic
and said,
'I'm thinking of taking him out of hock.
I pawned him years ago.'
Who would buy?
The pawned demon,
Yellowing with forgetfulness
and hand at his throat?
Take him out of hock, my friend,
but beware of the grief
that will fly into your mouth like a bird.
My demon,
too often undressed,
too often a crucifix I bring forth,
too often a dead daisy I give water to
too often the child I give birth to
and then abort, nameless, nameless...
earthless.
Oh demon within,
I am afraid and seldom put my hand up
to my mouth and stitch it up
covering you, smothering you
from the public voyeury eyes
of my typewriter keys.
If I should pawn you,
what bullion would they give for you,
what pennies, swimming in their copper kisses

what bird on its way to perishing?
No.
No.

I accept you,
you come with the dead who people my dreams,
who walk all over my desk
(as in Mother, cancer blossoming on her
Best & Co. titswaltzing
with her tissue paper ghost)
the dead, who give sweets to the diabetic in me,
who give bolts to the seizure of roses
that sometimes fly in and out of me.
Yes.
Yes.
I accept you, demon.
I will not cover your mouth.
If it be man I love, apple laden and foul
or if it be woman I love, sick unto her blood
and its sugary gasses and tumbling branches.
Demon come forth,
even if it be God I call forth
standing like a carrion,
wanting to eat me,
starting at the lips and tongue.
And me wanting to glide into His spoils,
I take bread and wine,
and the demon farts and giggles,
at my letting God out of my mouth
anonymous woman
at the anonymous altar.

Despair

Who is he?
A railroad track toward hell?
Breaking like a stick of furniture?
The hope that suddenly overflows the cesspool?
The love that goes down the drain like spit?
The love that said forever, forever
and then runs you over like a truck?
Are you a prayer that floats into a radio advertisement?
Despair,
I don't like you very well.
You don't suit my clothes or my cigarettes.
Why do you locate here
as large as a tank,
aiming at one half of a lifetime?
Couldn't you just go float into a tree
instead of locating here at my roots,
forcing me out of the life I've led
when it's been my belly so long?
All right!
I'll take you along on the trip
where for so many years
my arms have been speechless

61

Doctors
They work with herbs
and penicillin
They work with gentleness
and the scalpel.
They dig out the cancer,
close an incision
and say a prayer
to the poverty of the skin.

They are not Gods
though they would like to be;
they are only a human
trying to fix up a human.
Many humans die.
They die like the tender,
palpitating berries
in November.
But all along the doctors remember:
First do no harm.
They would kiss if it would heal.
It would not heal.
If the doctors cure
then the sun sees it.
If the doctors kill
then the earth hides it.
The doctors should fear arrogance
more than cardiac arrest.
If they are too proud,
and some are,
then they leave home on horseback
but God returns them on foot.

Doors, Doors, Doors

1. Old Man

Old man, it's four flights up and for what?
Your room is hardly bigger than your bed.
Puffing as you climb, you are a brown woodcut
stooped over the thin tail and the wornout tread.
The room will do. All that's left of the old life
is jampacked on shelves from floor to ceiling
like a supermarket: your books, your dead wife
generously fat in her polished frame, the congealing
bowl of cornflakes sagging in their instant milk,
your hot plate and your one luxury, a telephone.
You leave your door open, lounging in maroon silk
and smiling at the other roomers who live alone.
Well, almost alone. Through the old-fashioned wall
the fellow next door has a girl who comes to call.
Twice a week at noon during their lunch hour
they puase by your door to peer into your world.
They speak sadly as if the wine they carry would sour
or as if the mattress would not keep them curled
together, extravagantly young in their tight lock.
Old man, you are their father holding court
in the dingy hall until their alarm clock
rings and unwinds them. You unstopper the quart
of brandy you've saved, examining the small print
in the telephone book. The phone in your lap is all
that's left of your family name. Like a Romanoff prince
you stay the same in your small alcove off the hall.
Castaway, your time is a flat sea that doesn't stop,
with no new land to make for and no
new stories to swap.

2. Seamstress

I'm at pains to know what else I could have done

but move him out of his parish, him being my son;
him being the only one at home since his Pa
left us to beat the Japs at Okinawa.
I put the gold star up in the front window
beside the flag. Alterations is what I know
and what I did: hems, gussets and seams.
When my boy had the fever and the bad dreams
I paid for the clinic exam and a pack of lies.
As a youngster his private parts were undersize.
I thought of his Pa, that muscly old laugh he had
and the boy was thin as a moth, but never once bad,
as smart as a rooster! To hear some neighbors tell,
Your kid! He'll go far. He'll marry well.
So when he talked of taking the cloth, I thought
I'd talk him out of it. You're all I got,
I told him. For six years he studied up. I prayed
against God Himself for my boy. But he stayed.
Christ was a hornet inside his head. I guess
I'd better stitch the zipper in this dress.
I guess I'll get along. I always did.
Across the hall from me's an old invalid,
aside of him, a young one - he carries on
with a girl who pretends she comes to use the john.
The old one with the bad breath and his bed all mussed,
he smiles and talks to them. He's got some crust.
Sure as hell, what else could I have done
but pack up and move in here, him being my son?
3. Young Girl
Dear love, as simple as some distant evil
we walk a little drunk up these three flughts
where you tacked a Dufy print above your army cot.
The thin apartment doors on the way up will
not tell us. We are saying, we have our rights
and let them see the sandwiches and wine we bought
for we do not explain my husband's insane abuse

and we do not say why your wild-haired wife has fled
or that my father opened like a walnut and then was dead.
Your palms fold over me like knees. Love is the only use.
Both a little drunk in the afternoon
with the forgotten smart of August on our skin
we hold hands as if we were still children who trudge
up the wooden tower, on up past that close platoon
of doors, past the dear old man who always asks us in
and the one who sews like a wasp and will not budge.
Climbing the dark halls, I ignore their papers and pails,
the twelve coats of rubbish of someone else's dim life.
Tell them need is an excuse for love. Tell them need prevails.
Tell them I remake and smooth your bed and am your wife.

Dreaming The Breasts

Mother,
strange goddess face
above my milk home,
that delicate asylum,
I ate you up.
All my need took
you down like a meal.
What you gave
I remember in a dream:
the freckled arms binding me,
the laugh somewhere over my woolly hat,
the blood fingers tying my shoe,
the breasts hanging like two bats
and then darting at me,
bending me down.
The breasts I knew at midnight
beat like the sea in me now.
Mother, I put bees in my mouth
to keep from eating
yet it did no good.
In the end they cut off your breasts
and milk poured from them
into the surgeon's hand
and he embraced them.
I took them from him
and planted them.
I have put a padlock
on you, Mother, dear dead human,
so that your great bells,
those dear white ponies,

can go galloping, galloping,
wherever you are.

Earthworm

Slim inquirer, while the old fathers sleep
you are reworking their soil, you have
a grocery store there down under the earth
and it is well stocked with broken wine bottles,
old cigars, old door knobs and earth,
that great brown flour that you kiss each day.
There are dark stars in the cool evening and
you fondle them like killer birds' beaks.
But what I want to know is why when small boys
dig you up for curiosity and cut you in half
why each half lives and crawls away as if whole.
Have you no beginning and end? Which heart is
the real one? Which eye the seer? Why
is it in the infinite plan that you would
be severed and rise from the dead like a gargoyle
with two heads?

Elegy In The Classroom

In the thin classroom, where your face
was noble and your words were all things,
I find this boily creature in your place;
find you disarranged, squatting on the window sill,
irrefutably placed up there,
like a hunk of some big frog
watching us through the V
of your woolen legs.
Even so, I must admire your skill.
You are so gracefully insane.
We fidget in our plain chairs
and pretend to catalogue
our facts for your burly sorcery
or ignore your fat blind eyes
or the prince you ate yesterday
who was wise, wise, wise.

Elizabeth Gone

1.
You lay in the nest of your real death,
Beyond the print of my nervous fingers
Where they touched your moving head;
Your old skin puckering, your lungs' breath
Grown baby short as you looked up last
At my face swinging over the human bed,
And somewhere you cried, let me go let me go.
You lay in the crate of your last death,
But were not you, not finally you.
They have stuffed her cheeks, I said;
This clay hand, this mask of Elizabeth
Are not true. From within the satin
And the suede of this inhuman bed,
Something cried, let me go let me go.
2.
They gave me your ash and bony shells,
Rattling like gourds in the cardboard urn,
Rattling like stones that their oven had blest.
I waited you in the cathedral of spells
And I waited you in the country of the living,
Still with the urn crooned to my breast,
When something cried, let me go let me go.
So I threw out your last bony shells
And heard me scream for the look of you,
Your apple face, the simple creche
Of your arms, the August smells
Of your skin. Then I sorted your clothes
And the loves you had left, Elizabeth,
Elizabeth, until you were gone.

End, Middle, Beginning

There was an unwanted child.
Aborted by three modern methods
she hung on to the womb,
hooked onto I
building her house into it
and it was to no avail,
to black her out.
At her birth
she did not cry,
spanked indeed,
but did not yellinstead
snow fell out of her mouth.
As she grew, year by year,
her hair turned like a rose in a vase,
and bled down her face.
Rocks were placed on her to keep
the growing silent,
and though they bruised,
they did not kill,
though kill was tangled into her beginning.
They locked her in a football
but she merely curled up
and pretended it was a warm doll's house.
They pushed insects in to bite her off
and she let them crawl into her eyes
pretending they were a puppet show.
Later, later,
grown fully, as they say,
they gave her a ring,
and she wore it like a root
and said to herself,
'To be not loved is the human condition,'

and lay like a stature in her bed.
Then once,
by terrible chance,
love took her in his big boat
and she shoveled the ocean
in a scalding joy.
Then,
slowly,
love seeped away,
the boat turned into paper
and she knew her fate,
at last.
Turn where you belong,
into a deaf mute
that metal house,
let him drill you into no one.

Flee On Your Donkey

Because there was no other place
to flee to,
I came back to the scene of the disordered senses,
came back last night at midnight,
arriving in the thick June night
without luggage or defenses,
giving up my car keys and my cash,
keeping only a pack of Salem cigarettes
the way a child holds on to a toy.
I signed myself in where a stranger
puts the inked-in X's—
for this is a mental hospital,
not a child's game.
Today an intern knocks my knees,
testing for reflexes.
Once I would have winked and begged for dope.
Today I am terribly patient.
Today crows play black-jack
on the stethoscope.
Everyone has left me
except my muse,
that good nurse.
She stays in my hand,
a mild white mouse.
The curtains, lazy and delicate,
billow and flutter and drop
like the Victorian skirts
of my two maiden aunts
who kept an antique shop.
Hornets have been sent.
They cluster like floral arrangements on the screen.
Hornets, dragging their thin stingers,
hover outside, all knowing,

hissing: the hornet knows.
I heard it as a child
but what was it that he meant?
The hornet knows!
What happened to Jack and Doc and Reggy?
Who remembers what lurks in the heart of man?
What did The Green Hornet mean, he knows?
Or have I got it wrong?
Is it The Shadow who had seen
me from my bedside radio?
Now it's Dinn, Dinn, Dinn!
while the ladies in the next room argue
and pick their teeth.
Upstairs a girl curls like a snail;
in another room someone tries to eat a shoe;
meanwhile an adolescent pads up and down
the hall in his white tennis socks.
A new doctor makes rounds
advertising tranquilizers, insulin, or shock
to the uninitiated.
Six years of such small preoccupations!
Six years of shuttling in and out of this place!
O my hunger! My hunger!
I could have gone around the world twice
or had new children - all boys.
It was a long trip with little days in it
and no new places.
In here,
it's the same old crowd,
the same ruined scene.
The alcoholic arrives with his gold clubs.
The suicide arrives with extra pills sewn
into the lining of her dress.
The permanent guests have done nothing new.
Their faces are still small

like babies with jaundice.
Meanwhile,
they carried out my mother,
wrapped like somebody's doll, in sheets,
bandaged her jaw and stuffed up her holes.
My father, too. He went out on the rotten blood
he used up on other women in the Middle West.
He went out, a cured old alcoholic
on crooked feet and useless hands.
He went out calling for his father
who died all by himself long ago -
that fat banker who got locked up,
his genes suspended like dollars,
wrapped up in his secret,
tied up securely in a straitjacket.
But you, my doctor, my enthusiast,
were better than Christ;
you promised me another world
to tell me who
I was.
I spent most of my time,
a stranger,
damned and in trance—that little hut,
that naked blue-veined place,
my eyes shut on the confusing office,
eyes circling into my childhood,
eyes newly cut.
Years of hints
strung out—a serialized case history—
thirty-three years of the same dull incest
that sustained us both.
You, my bachelor analyst,
who sat on Marlborough Street,
sharing your office with your mother
and giving up cigarettes each New Year,

were the new God,
the manager of the Gideon Bible.
I was your third-grader
with a blue star on my forehead.
In trance I could be any age,
voice, gesture—all turned backward
like a drugstore clock.
Awake, I memorized dreams.
Dreams came into the ring
like third string fighters,
each one a bad bet
who might win
because there was no other.
I stared at them,
concentrating on the abyss
the way one looks down into a rock quarry,
uncountable miles down,
my hands swinging down like hooks
to pull dreams up out of their cage.
O my hunger! My hunger!
Once, outside your office,
I collapsed in the old-fashioned swoon
between the illegally parked cars.
I threw myself down,
pretending dead for eight hours.
I thought I had died
into a snowstorm.
Above my head
chains cracked along like teeth
digging their way through the snowy street.
I lay there
like an overcoat
that someone had thrown away.
You carried me back in,
awkwardly, tenderly,

with help of the red-haired secretary
who was built like a lifeguard.
My shoes,
I remember,
were lost in the snowbank
as if I planned never to walk again.
That was the winter
that my mother died,
half mad on morphine,
blown up, at last,
like a pregnant pig.
I was her dreamy evil eye.
In fact,

75

I carried a knife in my pocketbook—
my husband's good L. L. Bean hunting knife.
I wasn't sure if I should slash a tire
or scrape the guts out of some dream.
You taught me
to believe in dreams;
thus I was the dredger.
I held them like an old woman with arthritic fingers,
carefully straining the water out—
sweet dark playthings,
and above all, mysterious
until they grew mournful and weak.
O my hunger! My hunger!
I was the one
who opened the warm eyelid
like a surgeon
and brought forth young girls
to grunt like fish.
I told you,
I said—
but I was lying—

that the knife was for my mother . . .
and then I delivered her.
The curtains flutter out
and slump against the bars.
They are my two thin ladies
named Blanche and Rose.
The grounds outside
are pruned like an estate at Newport.
Far off, in the field,
something yellow grows.
Was it last month or last year
that the ambulance ran like a hearse
with its siren blowing on suicide—
Dinn, dinn, dinn!—
a noon whistle that kept insisting on life
all the way through the traffic lights?
I have come back
but disorder is not what it was.
I have lost the trick of it!
The innocence of it!
That fellow-patient in his stovepipe hat
with his fiery joke, his manic smile—
even he seems blurred, small and pale.
I have come back,
recommitted,
fastened to the wall like a bathroom plunger,
held like a prisoner
who was so poor
he fell in love with jail.
I stand at this old window
complaining of the soup,
examining the grounds,
allowing myself the wasted life.
Soon I will raise my face for a white flag,
and when God enters the fort,

I won't spit or gag on his finger.
I will eat it like a white flower.
Is this the old trick, the wasting away,
the skull that waits for its dose
of electric power?
This is madness
but a kind of hunger.
What good are my questions
in this hierarchy of death
where the earth and the stones go
Dinn! Dinn! Dinn!
It is hardly a feast.
It is my stomach that makes me suffer.
Turn, my hungers!
For once make a deliberate decision.
There are brains that rot here
like black bananas.
Hearts have grown as flat as dinner plates.
Anne, Anne,
flee on your donkey,
flee this sad hotel,
ride out on some hairy beast,
gallop backward pressing
your buttocks to his withers,
sit to his clumsy gait somehow.
Ride out
any old way you please!
In this place everyone talks to his own mouth.
That's what it means to be crazy.
Those I loved best died of it—
the fool's disease.

For God While Sleeping

Sleeping in fever, I am unfair
to know just who you are:
hung up like a pig on exhibit,
the delicate wrists,
the beard drooling blood and vinegar;
hooked to your own weight,
jolting toward death under your nameplate.
Everyone in this crowd needs a bath.
I am dressed in rags.
The mother wears blue.
You grind your teeth
and with each new breath
your jaws gape and your diaper sags.
I am not to blame
for all this. I do not know your name.
Skinny man, you are somebody's fault.
You ride on dark poles -
a wooden bird that a trader built
for some fool who felt
that he could make the flight. Now you roll
in your sleep, seasick
on your own breathing, poor old convict.

For John, Who Begs Me Not To Enquire Further

Not that it was beautiful,
but that, in the end, there was
a certain sense of order there;
something worth learning
in that narrow diary of my mind,
in the commonplaces of the asylum
where the cracked mirror
or my own selfish death
outstared me.
And if I tried
to give you something else,
something outside of myself,
you would not know
that the worst of anyone
can be, finally,
an accident of hope.
I tapped my own head;
it was a glass, an inverted bowl.
It is a small thing
to rage in your own bowl.
At first it was private.
Then it was more than myself;
it was you, or your house
or your kitchen.
And if you turn away
because there is no lesson here
I will hold my awkward bowl,
with all its cracked stars shining
like a complicated lie,
and fasten a new skin around it
as if I were dressing an orange

or a strange sun.
Not that it was beautiful,
but that I found some order there.
There ought to be something special
for someone
in this kind of hope.
This is something I would never find
in a lovelier place, my dear,
although your fear is anyone's fear,
like an invisible veil between us all…
and sometimes in private,
my kitchen, your kitchen,
my face, your face.

For Johnny Pole On The Forgotten Beach

In his tenth July some instinct
taught him to arm the waiting wave,
a giant where its mouth hung open.
He rode on the lip that buoyed him there
and buckled him under. The beach was strung
with children paddling their ages in,
under the glare od noon chipping
its light out. He stood up, anonymous
and straight among them, between
their sand pails and nursery crafts.
The breakers cartwheeled in and over
to puddle their toes and test their perfect
skin. He was my brother, my small
Johnny brother, almost ten. We flopped
down upon a towel to grind the sand
under us and watched the Atlantic sea
move fire, like night sparklers;
and lost our weight in the festival
season. He dreamed, he said, to be
a man designed like a balanced wave…
how someday he would wait, giant
and straight.
Johnny, your dream moves summers
inside my mind.
He was tall and twenty that July,
but there was no balance to help;
only the shells came straight and even.
This was the first beach of assault;
the odor of death hung in the air
like rotting potatoes, the junkyard
of landing craft waited open and rusting.
The bodies were strung out as if they were

still reaching for each other, where they lay
to blacken, to burst through their perfect
skin. And Johnny Pole was one of them.
He gave in like a small wave, a sudden
hole in his belly and the years all gone
where the Pacific noon chipped its light out.
Like a bean bag, outflung, head loose
and anonymous, he lay. Did the sea move fire
for its battle season? Does he lie there
forever, where his rifle waits, giant
and straight?…I think you die again
and live again,
Johnny, each summer that moves inside
my mind.

For My Lover, Returning To His Wife

She is all there.
She was melted carefully down for you
and cast up from your childhood,
cast up from your one hundred favorite aggies.
She has always been there, my darling.
She is, in fact, exquisite.
Fireworks in the dull middle of February
and as real as a cast-iron pot.
Let's face it, I have been momentary.
vA luxury. A bright red sloop in the harbor.
My hair rising like smoke from the car window.
Littleneck clams out of season.
She is more than that. She is your have to have,
has grown you your practical your tropical growth.
This is not an experiment. She is all harmony.
She sees to oars and oarlocks for the dinghy,
has placed wild flowers at the window at breakfast,
sat by the potter's wheel at midday,
set forth three children under the moon,
three cherubs drawn by Michelangelo,
done this with her legs spread out
in the terrible months in the chapel.
If you glance up, the children are there
like delicate balloons resting on the ceiling.
She has also carried each one down the hall
after supper, their heads privately bent,
two legs protesting, person to person,
her face flushed with a song and their little sleep.
I give you back your heart.
I give you permission -
for the fuse inside her, throbbing

angrily in the dirt, for the bitch in her
and the burying of her wound -
for the burying of her small red wound alive -
for the pale flickering flare under her ribs,
for the drunken sailor who waits in her left pulse,
for the mother's knee, for the stocking,
for the garter belt, for the call -
the curious call
when you will burrow in arms and breasts
and tug at the orange ribbon in her hair
and answer the call, the curious call.
She is so naked and singular
She is the sum of yourself and your dream.
Climb her like a monument, step after step.
She is solid.
As for me, I am a watercolor.
I wash off.

For The Year Of The Insane

A prayer

O Mary, fragile mother,
hear me, hear me now
although I do not know your words.
The black rosary with its silver Christ
lies unblessed in my hand
for I am the unbeliever.
Each bead is round and hard between my fingers,
a small black angel.
O Mary, permit me this grace,
this crossing over,
although I am ugly,
submerged in my own past
and my own madness.
Although there are chairs
I lie on the floor.
Only my hands are alive,
touching beads.
Word for word, I stumble.
A beginner, I feel your mouth touch mine.
I count beads as waves,
hammering in upon me.
I am ill at their numbers,
sick, sick in the summer heat
and the window above me
is my only listener, my awkward being.
She is a large taker, a soother.
The giver of breath
she murmurs,
exhaling her wide lung like an enormous fish.
Closer and closer
comes the hour of my death

as I rearrange my face, grow back,
grow undeveloped and straight-haired.
All this is death.
In the mind there is a thin alley called death
and I move through it as
through water.
My body is useless.
It lies, curled like a dog on the carpet.
It has given up.
There are no words here except the half-learned,
the Hail Mary and the full of grace.
Now I have entered the year without words.
I note the queer entrance and the exact voltage.
Without words they exist.
Without words on my touch bread
and be handed bread
and make no sound.
O Mary, tender physician,
come with powders and herbs
for I am in the center.
It is very small and the air is gray
as in a steam house.
I am handed wine as a child is handed milk.
It is presented in a delicate glass
with a round bowl and a thin lip.
The wine itself is pitch-colored, musty and secret.
The glass rises in its own toward my mouth
and I notice this and understand this
only because it has happened.
I have this fear of coughing
but I do not speak,
a fear of rain, a fear of the horseman
who comes riding into my mouth.
The glass tilts in on its own
and I amon fire.

I see two thin streaks burn down my chin.
I see myself as one would see another.
I have been cut int two.
O Mary, open your eyelids.
I am in the domain of silence,
the kingdom of the crazy and the sleeper.
There is blood here.
and I haven't eaten it.
O mother of the womb,
did I come for blood alone?
O little mother,
I am in my own mind.
I am locked in the wrong house.

Funnel

The family story tells, and it was told true,
of my great-grandfather who begat eight
genius children and bought twelve almost-new
grand pianos. He left a considerable estate
when he died. The children honored their
separate arts; two became moderately famous,
three married and fattened their delicate share
of wealth and brilliance. The sixth one was
a concert pianist. She had a notable career
and wore cropped hair and walked like a man,
or so I heard when prying a childhood car
into the hushed talk of the straight Maine clan.
One died a pinafore child, she stays her five
years forever. And here is one that wrote-
I sort his odd books and wonder his once alive
words and scratch out my short marginal notes
and finger my accounts.
back from that great-grandfather I have come
to tidy a country graveyard for his sake,
to chat with the custodian under a yearly sun
and touch a ghost sound where it lies awake.
I like best to think of that Bunyan man
slapping his thighs and trading the yankee sale
for one dozen grand pianos. it fit his plan
of culture to do it big. On this same scale
he built seven arking houses and they still stand.
One, five stories up, straight up like a square
box, still dominates its coastal edge of land.
It is rented cheap in the summer musted air
to sneaker-footed families who pad through
its rooms and sometimes finger the yellow keys
of an old piano that wheezes bells of mildew.

Like a shoe factory amid the spruce trees
it squats; flat roof and rows of windows spying
through the mist. Where those eight children danced
their starfished summers, the thirty-six pines sighing,
that bearded man walked giant steps and chanced
his gifts in numbers.
Back from that great-grandfather I have come
to puzzle a bending gravestone for his sake,
to question this diminishing and feed a minimum
of children their careful slice of suburban cake.

Ghosts

Some ghosts are women,
neither abstract nor pale,
their breasts as limp as killed fish.
Not witches, but ghosts
who come, moving their useless arms
like forsaken servants.
Not all ghosts are women,
I have seen others;
fat, white-bellied men,
wearing their genitals like old rags.
Not devils, but ghosts.
This one thumps barefoot, lurching
above my bed.
But that isn't all.
Some ghosts are children.
Not angels, but ghosts;
curling like pink tea cups
on any pillow, or kicking,
showing their innocent bottoms, wailing
for Lucifer.

Gods

Ms. Sexton went out looking for the gods.
She began looking in the sky
—expecting a large white angel with a blue crotch.
No one.
She looked next in all the learned books
and the print spat back at her.
No one
She made a pilgrimage to the great poet
and he belched in her face.
No one.
She prayed in all the churches of the world
and learned a great deal about culture.
No one.
She went to the Atlantic, the Pacific, for surely God…
No one.
She went to the Buddha, the Brahma, the Pyramids
and found immense postcards.
No one.
Then she journeyed back to her own house
and the gods of the world were shut in the lavatory.
At last!
she cried out,
and locked the door.

92

Going Gone
Over stone walls and barns,
miles from the black-eyed Susans,
over circus tents and moon rockets
you are going, going.
You who have inhabited me
in the deepest and most broken place,

are going, going.
An old woman calls up to you
from her deathbed deep in sores,
asking, 'What do you keep of her?'
She is the crone in the fables.
She is the fool at the supper
and you, sir, are the traveler.
Although you are in a hurry
you stop to open a small basket
and under layers of petticoats
you show her the tiger-striped eyes
that you have lately plucked,
you show her specialty, the lips,
those two small bundles,
you show her the two hands
that grip her fiercely,
one being mine, one being yours.
Torn right off at the wrist bone
when you started in your
impossible going, gone.
Then you place the basket
in the old woman's hollow lap
and as a last act she fondles
these artifacts like a child's head
and murmurs, 'Precious. Precious.'
And you are glad you have given
them to this one for she too
is making a trip.

Her Kind

have gone out, a possessed witch,
haunting the black air, braver at night;
dreaming evil, I have done my hitch
over the plain houses, light by light:
lonely thing, twelve-fingered, out of mind.
A woman like that is not a woman, quite.
I have been her kind.

I have found the warm caves in the woods,
filled them with skillets, carvings, shelves,
closets, silks, innumerable goods;
fixed the suppers for the worms and the elves:
whining, rearranging the disaligned.
A woman like that is misunderstood.
I have been her kind.

I have ridden in your cart, driver,
waved my nude arms at villages going by,
learning the last bright routes, survivor
where your flames still bite my thigh
and my ribs crack where your wheels wind.
A woman like that is not ashamed to die.
I have been her kind.

Hornet

A red-hot needle
hangs out of him, he steers by it
as if it were a rudder, he
would get in the house any way he could
and then he would bounce from window
to ceiling, buzzing and looking for you.
Do not sleep for he is there wrapped in the curtain.
Do not sleep for he is there under the shelf.
Do not sleep for he wants to sew up your skin,
he want to leap into your body like a hammer
with a nail, do not sleep he wants to get into
your nose and make a transplant, he wants do not
sleep he wants to bury your fur and make
a nest of knives, he wants to slide under your
fingernail and push in a splinter, do not sleep
he wants to climb out of the toilet when you sit on it
and make a home in the embarrassed hair do not sleep
he wants you to walk into him as into a dark fire.

Housewife

Some women marry houses.
It's another kind of skin; it has a heart,
a mouth, a liver and bowel movements.
The walls are permanent and pink.
See how she sits on her knees all day,
faithfully washing herself down.
Men enter by force, drawn back like Jonah
into their fleshy mothers.
A woman is her mother.
That's the main thing.

Hurry Up Please It's Time

What is death, I ask.
What is life, you ask.
I give them both my buttocks,
my two wheels rolling off toward Nirvana.
They are neat as a wallet,
opening and closing on their coins,
the quarters, the nickels,
straight into the crapper.
Why shouldn't I pull down my pants
and moon the executioner
as well as paste raisins on my breasts?
Why shouldn't I pull down my pants
and show my little cunny to Tom
and Albert? They wee-wee funny.
I wee-wee like a squaw.
I have ink but no pen, still
I dream that I can piss in God's eye.
I dream I'm a boy with a zipper.
It's so practical, la de dah.
The trouble with being a woman, Skeezix,
is being a little girl in the first place.
Not all the books of the world will change that.
I have swallowed an orange, being woman.
You have swallowed a ruler, being man.
Yet waiting to die we are the same thing.
Jehovah pleasures himself with his axe
before we are both overthrown.
Skeezix, you are me. La de dah.
You grow a beard but our drool is identical.
Forgive us, Father, for we know not.
Today is November 14th, 1972.
I live in Weston, Mass., Middlesex County,

U.S.A., and it rains steadily
in the pond like white puppy eyes.
The pond is waiting for its skin.
the pond is waiting for its leather.
The pond is waiting for December and its Novocain.

It begins:
Interrogator:
What can you say of your last seven days?
Anne:
They were tired.
Interrogator:
One day is enough to perfect a man.
Anne:
I watered and fed the plant.
*

My undertaker waits for me.
he is probably twenty-three now,
learning his trade.
He'll stitch up the gren,
he'll fasten the bones down
lest they fly away.
I am flying today.
I am not tired today.
I am a motor.
I am cramming in the sugar.
I am running up the hallways.
I am squeezing out the milk.
I am dissecting the dictionary.
I am God, la de dah.
Peanut butter is the American food.
We all eat it, being patriotic.
Ms. Dog is out fighting the dollars,
rolling in a field of bucks.
You've got it made if you take the wafer,

take some wine,
take some bucks,
the green papery song of the office.
What a jello she could make with it,
the fives, the tens, the twenties,

all in a goo to feed the baby.
Andrew Jackson as an hors d'oeuvre,
la de dah.
I wish I were the U.S. Mint,
turning it all out,
turtle green
and monk black.
Who's that at the podium
in black and white,
blurting into the mike?
Ms. Dog.
Is she spilling her guts?
You bet.
Otherwise they cough…
The day is slipping away, why am I
out here, what do they want?
I am sorrowful in November…
(no they don't want that,
they want bee stings).
Toot, toot, tootsy don't cry.
Toot, toot, tootsy good-bye.
If you don't get a letter then
you'll know I'm in jail…
Remember that, Skeezix,
our first song?
Who's thinking those things?
Ms. Dog! She's out fighting the dollars.
Milk is the American drink.
Oh queens of sorrows,

oh water lady,
place me in your cup
and pull over the clouds
so no one can see.
She don't want no dollars.
She done want a mama.
The white of the white.
Anne says:
This is the rainy season.
I am sorrowful in November.
The kettle is whistling.
I must butter the toast.
And give it jam too.
My kitchen is a heart.
I must feed it oxygen once in a while
and mother the mother.
                                    *

Say the woman is forty-four.
Say she is five seven-and-a-half.
Say her hair is stick color.
Say her eyes are chameleon.
Would you put her in a sack and bury her,
suck her down into the dumb dirt?
Some would.
If not, time will.
Ms. Dog, how much time you got left?
Ms. Dog, when you gonna feel that cold nose?
You better get straight with the Maker
cuz it's coming, it's a coming!
The cup of coffee is growing and growing
and they're gonna stick your little doll's head
into it and your lungs a gonna get paid
and your clothes a gonna melt.
Hear that, Ms. Dog!
You of the songs,

you of the classroom,
you of the pocketa-pocketa,
you hungry mother,
you spleen baby!
Them angels gonna be cut down like wheat.
Them songs gonna be sliced with a razor.
Them kitchens gonna get a boulder in the belly.
Them phones gonna be torn out at the root.
There's power in the Lord, baby,
and he's gonna turn off the moon.
He's gonna nail you up in a closet
and there'll be no more Atlantic,
no more dreams, no more seeds.
One noon as you walk out to the mailbox
He'll snatch you up -
a wopman beside the road like a red mitten.

There's a sack over my head.
I can't see. I'm blind.
The sea collapses.
The sun is a bone.
Hi-ho the derry-o,
we all fall down.
If I were a fisherman I could comprehend.
They fish right through the door
and pull eyes from the fire.
They rock upon the daybreak
and amputate the waters.
They are beating the sea,
they are hurting it,
delving down into the inscrutable salt.
*

When mother left the room
and left me in the big black
and sent away my kitty

to be fried in the camps
and took away my blanket
to wash the me out of it
I lay in the soiled cold and prayed.
It was a little jail in which
I was never slapped with kisses.
I was the engine that couldn't.
Cold wigs blew on the trees outside
and car lights flew like roosters
on the ceiling.
Cradle, you are a grave place.
Interrogator:
What color is the devil?
Anne:
Black and blue.
Interrogator:
What goes up the chimney?

Anne:
Fat Lazarus in his red suit.
Forgive us, Father, for we know not.
Ms. Dog prefers to sunbathe nude.
Let the indifferent sky look on.
So what!
Let Mrs. Sewal pull the curtain back,
from her second story.
So what!
Let United Parcel Service see my parcel.
La de dah.
Sun, you hammer of yellow,
you hat on fire,
you honeysuckle mama,
pour your blonde on me!
Let me laugh for an entire hour
at your supreme being, your Cadillac stuff,

because I've come a long way
from Brussels sprouts.
I've come a long way to peel off my clothes
and lay me down in the grass.
Once only my palms showed.
Once I hung around in my woolly tank suit,
drying my hair in those little meatball curls.
Now I am clothed in gold air with
one dozen halos glistening on my skin.
I am a fortunate lady.
I've gotten out of my pouch
and my teeth are glad
and my heart, that witness,
beats well at the thought.
Oh body, be glad.
You are good goods.
*

Middle-class lady,
you make me smile.
You dig a hole

and come out with a sunburn.
If someone hands you a glass of water
you start constructing a sailboat.
If someone hands you a candy wrapper,
you take it to the book binder.
Pocketa-pocketa.
Once upon a time Ms. Dog was sixty-six.
She had white hair and wrinkles deep as splinters.
her portrait was nailed up like Christ
and she said of it:
That's when I was forty-two,
down in Rockport with a hat on for the sun,
and Barbara drew a line drawing.
We were, at that moment, drinking vodka

and ginger beer and there was a chill in the air,
although it was July, and she gave me her sweater
to bundle up in. The next summer Skeezix tied
strings in that hat when we were fishing in Maine.
(It had gone into the lake twice.)
Of such moments is happiness made.
Forgive us, Father, for we know not.
Once upon a time we were all born,
popped out like jelly rolls
forgetting our fishdom,
the pleasuring seas,
the country of comfort,
spanked into the oxygens of death,
Good morning life, we say when we wake,
hail mary coffee toast
and we Americans take juice,
a liquid sun going down.
Good morning life.
To wake up is to be born.
To brush your teeth is to be alive.
To make a bowel movement is also desireable.
La de dah,
it's all routine.
Often there are wars
yet the shops keep open

and sausages are still fried.
People rub someone.
People copulate
entering each other's blood,
tying each other's tendons in knots,
transplanting their lives into the bed.
It doesn't matter if there are wars,
the business of life continues
unless you're the one that gets it.

Mama, they say, as their intestines
leak out. Even without wars
life is dangerous.
Boats spring leaks.
Cigarettes explode.
The snow could be radioactive.
Cancer could ooze out of the radio.
Who knows?
Ms. Dog stands on the shore
and the sea keeps rocking in
and she wants to talk to God.
Interrogator:
Why talk to God?
Anne:
It's better than playing bridge.
*

Learning to talk is a complex business.
My daughter's first word was utta,
meaning button.
Before there are words
do you dream?
In utero
do you dream?
Who taught you to suck?
And how come?
You don't need to be taught to cry.
The soul presses a button.
Is the cry saying something?
Does it mean help?

Or hello?
The cry of a gull is beautiful
and the cry of a crow is ugly
but what I want to know
is whether they mean the same thing.

Somewhere a man sits with indigestion
and he doesn't care.
A woman is buying bracelets
and earrings and she doesn't care.
La de dah.
Forgive us, Father, for we know not.
There are stars and faces.
There is ketchup and guitars.
There is the hand of a small child
when you're crossing the street.
There is the old man's last words:
More light! More light!
Ms. Dog wouldn't give them her buttocks.
She wouldn't moon at them.
Just at the killers of the dream.
The bus boys of the soul.
Or at death
who wants to make her a mummy.
And you too!
Wants to stuf her in a cold shoe
and then amputate the foot.
And you too!
La de dah.
What's the point of fighting the dollars
when all you need is a warm bed?
When the dog barks you let him in.
All we need is someone to let us in.
And one other thing:
to consider the lilies in the field.
Of course earth is a stranger, we pull at its
arms and still it won't speak.
The sea is worse.
It comes in, falling to its knees
but we can't translate the language.
It is only known that they are here to worship,

to worship the terror of the rain,
the mud and all its people,
the body itself,
working like a city,
the night and its slow blood
the autumn sky, mary blue.
but more than that,
to worship the question itself,
though the buildings burn
and the big people topple over in a faint.
Bring a flashlight, Ms. Dog,
and look in every corner of the brain
and ask and ask and ask
until the kingdom,
however queer,
will come.

Hutch

of her arms, this was her sin:
where the wood berries bin
of forest was new and full,
she crept out by its tall
posts, those wooden legs,
and heard the sound of wild pigs.
calling and did not wait nor care.
The leaves wept in her hair
as she sank to a pit of needles
and twisted out the ivyless
gate, where the wood berries bin
was full and a pig came in.

I Remember

By the first of August
the invisible beetles began
to snore and the grass was
as tough as hemp and was
no color——no more than
the sand was a color and
we had worn our bare feet
bare since the twentieth
of June and there were times
we forgot to wind up your
alarm clock and some nights
we took our gin warm and neat
from old jelly glasses while
the sun blew out of sight
like a red picture hat and
one day I tied my hair back
with a ribbon and you said
that I looked almost like
a puritan lady and what
I remember best is that
the door to your room was
the door to mine.

In Celebration Of My Uterus

Everyone in me is a bird.
I am beating all my wings.
They wanted to cut you out
but they will not.
They said you were immeasurably empty
but you are not.
They said you were sick unto dying
but they were wrong.
You are singing like a school girl.
You are not torn.
Sweet weight,
in celebration of the woman I am
and of the soul of the woman I am
and of the central creature and its delight
I sing for you. I dare to live.
Hello, spirit. Hello, cup.
Fasten, cover. Cover that does contain.
Hello to the soil of the fields.
Welcome, roots.
Each cell has a life.
There is enough here to please a nation.
It is enough that the populace own these goods.
Any person, any commonwealth would say of it,
"It is good this year that we may plant again
and think forward to a harvest.
A blight had been forecast and has been cast out."
Many women are singing together of this:
one is in a shoe factory cursing the machine,
one is at the aquarium tending a seal,
one is dull at the wheel of her Ford,
one is at the toll gate collecting,
one is tying the cord of a calf in Arizona,

one is straddling a cello in Russia,
one is shifting pots on the stove in Egypt,
one is painting her bedroom walls moon color,
one is dying but remembering a breakfast,
one is stretching on her mat in Thailand,
one is wiping the ass of her child,
one is staring out the window of a train
in the middle of Wyoming and one is
anywhere and some are everywhere and all
seem to be singing, although some can not
sing a note.
Sweet weight,
in celebration of the woman I am
let me carry a ten-foot scarf,
let me drum for the nineteen-year-olds,
let me carry bowls for the offering
(if that is my part).
Let me study the cardiovascular tissue,
let me examine the angular distance of meteors,
let me suck on the stems of flowers
(if that is my part).
Let me make certain tribal figures
(if that is my part).
For this thing the body needs
let me sing
for the supper,
for the kissing,
for the correct
yes.

In Excelsis

It is half winter, half spring,
and Barbara and I are standing
confronting the ocean.
Its mouth is open very wide,
and it has dug up its green,
throwing it, throwing it at the shore.
You say it is angry.
I say it is like a kicked Madonna.
Its womb collapses, drunk with its fever.
We breathe in its fury.
I, the inlander,
am here with you for just a small space.
I am almost afraid,
so long gone from the sea.
I have seen her smooth as a cheek.
I have seen her easy,
doing her business,
lapping in.
I have seen her rolling her hoops of blue.
I have seen her tear the land off.
I have seen her drown me twice,
and yet not take me.
You tell me that as the green drains backward
it covers Britain,
but have you never stood on that shore
and seen it cover you?
We have come to worship,
the tongues of the surf are prayers,
and we vow,
the unspeakable vow.
Both silently.
Both differently.

I wish to enter her like a dream,
leaving my roots here on the beach
like a pan of knives.
And my past to unravel, with its knots and snarls,
and walk into ocean,
letting it explode over me
and outward, where I would drink the moon
and my clothes would slip away,
and I would sink into the great mother arms
I never had,
except here where the abyss
throws itself on the sand
blow by blow,
over and over,
and we stand on the shore
loving its pulse
as it swallows the stars,
and has since it all began
and will continue into oblivion,
past our knowing
and the wild toppling green that enters us today,
for a small time
in half winter, half spring.

In Memoriam

In Memoriam
What's missing is the eyeballs
in each of us, but it doesn't matter
because you've got the bucks, the bucks, the bucks.
You let me touch them, fondle the green faces
lick at their numbers and it lets you be
my 'Daddy!' 'Daddy!' and though I fought all alone
with molesters and crooks, I knew your money
would save me, your courage, your 'I've had
considerable experience as a soldier…
fighting to win millions for myself, it's true.
But I did win,' and me praying for 'our men out there'
just made it okay to be an orphan whose blood was no one's,
whose curls were hung up on a wire machine and electrified,
while you built and unbuilt intrigues called nations,
and did in the bad ones, always, always,
and always came at my perils, the black Christs of childhood,
always came when my heart stood naked in the street
and they threw apples at it or twelve-day-old-dead-fish.
'Daddy!' 'Daddy,' we all won that war,
when you sang me the money songs
Annie, Annie you sang
and I knew you drove a pure gold car
and put diamonds in you coke
for the crunchy sound, the adorable sound
and the moon too was in your portfolio,
as well as the ocean with its sleepy dead.
And I was always brave, wasn't I?
I never bled?
I never saw a man expose himself.
No. No.

I never saw a drunkard in his blubber.
I never let lightning go in one car and out the other.
And all the men out there were never to come.
Never, like a deluge, to swim over my breasts
and lay their lamps in my insides.
No. No.

Just me and my 'Daddy'
and his tempestuous bucks
rolling in them like corn flakes
and only the bad ones died.
But I died yesterday,
'Daddy,' I died,
swallowing the Nazi-Jap animal
and it won't get out
it keeps knocking at my eyes,
my big orphan eyes,
kicking! Until eyeballs pop out
and even my dog puts up his four feet
and lets go
of his military secret
with his big red tongue
flying up and down
like yours should have
as we board our velvet train.

In The Deep Museum

My God, my God, what queer corner am I in?
Didn't I die, blood running down the post,
lungs gagging for air, die there for the sin
of anyone, my sour mouth giving up the ghost?
Surely my body is done? Surely I died?
And yet, I know, I'm here. What place is this?
Cold and queer, I sting with life. I lied.
Yes, I lied. Or else in some damned cowardice
my body would not give me up. I touch
fine cloth with my hand and my cheeks are cold.
If this is hell, then hell could not be much,
neither as special or as ugly as I was told.
What's that I hear, snuffling and pawing its way
toward me? Its tongue knocks a pebble out of place
as it slides in, a sovereign. How can I pray>
It is panting; it is an odor with a face
like the skin of a donkey. It laps my sores.
It is hurt, I think, as a I touch its little head.
It bleeds. I have forgiven murderers and whores
and now must wait like old Jonah, not dead
nor alive, stroking a clumsy animal. A rat.
His teeth test me; he waits like a good cook,
knowing his own ground. I forgive him that,
as I forgave my Judas the money he took.
Now I hold his soft red sore to my lips
as his brothers crowd in, hairy angels who take
my gift. My ankles are a flute. I lose hips
and wrists. For three days, for love's sake,
I bless this other death. Oh, not in air -
in dirt. Under the rotting veins of its roots,
under the markets, under the sheep bed where

the hill is food, under the slippery fruits
of the vineyard, I go. Unto the bellies and jaws
of rats I commit my prophecy and fear.
Far below The Cross, I correct its flaws.
We have kept the miracle. I will not be here.

It Is A Spring Afternoon

Everything here is yellow and green.
Listen to its throat, its earthskin,
the bone dry voices of the peepers
as they throb like advertisements.
The small animals of the woods
are carrying their deathmasks
into a narrow winter cave.
The scarecrow has plucked out
his two eyes like diamonds
and walked into the village.
The general and the postman
have taken off their packs.
This has all happened before
but nothing here is obsolete.
Everything here is possible.
Because of this
perhaps a young girl has laid down
her winter clothes and has casually
placed herself upon a tree limb
that hangs over a pool in the river.
She has been poured out onto the limb,
low above the houses of the fishes
as they swim in and out of her reflection
and up and down the stairs of her legs.
Her body carries clouds all the way home.
She is overlooking her watery face
in the river where blind men
come to bathe at midday.
Because of this
the ground, that winter nightmare,
has cured its sores and burst
with green birds and vitamins.

Because of this
the trees turn in their trenches
and hold up little rain cups
by their slender fingers.
Because of this
a woman stands by her stove
singing and cooking flowers.
Everything here is yellow and green.
Surely spring will allow
a girl without a stitch on
to turn softly in her sunlight
and not be afraid of her bed.
She has already counted seven
blossoms in her green green mirror.
Two rivers combine beneath her.
The face of the child wrinkles.
in the water and is gone forever.
The woman is all that can be seen
in her animal loveliness.
Her cherished and obstinate skin
lies deeply under the watery tree.
Everything is altogether possible
and the blind men can also see.

Just Once

Just once I knew what life was for.
In Boston, quite suddenly, I understood;
walked there along the Charles River,
watched the lights copying themselves,
all neoned and strobe-hearted, opening
their mouths as wide as opera singers;
counted the stars, my little campaigners,
my scar daisies, and knew that I walked my love
on the night green side of it and cried
my heart to the eastbound cars and cried
my heart to the westbound cars and took
my truth across a small humped bridge
and hurried my truth, the charm of it, home
and hoarded these constants into morning
only to find them gone.

Killing The Love

I am the love killer,
I am murdering the music we thought so special,
that blazed between us, over and over.
I am murdering me, where I kneeled at your kiss.
I am pushing knives through the hands
that created two into one.
Our hands do not bleed at this,
they lie still in their dishonor.
I am taking the boats of our beds
and swamping them, letting them cough on the sea
and choke on it and go down into nothing.
I am stuffing your mouth with your
promises and watching
you vomit them out upon my face.
The Camp we directed?
I have gassed the campers.
Now I am alone with the dead,
flying off bridges,
hurling myself like a beer can into the wastebasket.
I am flying like a single red rose,
leaving a jet stream
of solitude
and yet I feel nothing,
though I fly and hurl,
my insides are empty
and my face is as blank as a wall.
Shall I call the funeral director?
He could put our two bodies into one pink casket,
those bodies from before,
and someone might send flowers,
and someone might come to mourn

and it would be in the obits,
and people would know that something died,
is no more, speaks no more, won't even
drive a car again and all of that.
When a life is over,

the one you were living for,
where do you go?
I'll work nights.
I'll dance in the city.
I'll wear red for a burning.
I'll look at the Charles very carefully,
wearing its long legs of neon.
And the cars will go by.
The cars will go by.
And there'll be no scream
from the lady in the red dress
dancing on her own Ellis Island,
who turns in circles,
dancing alone
as the cars go by.

Kind Sir: These Woods

Kind Sir: This is an old game
that we played when we were eight and ten.
Sometimes on The Island, in down Maine,
in late August, when the cold fog blew in
off the ocean, the forest between Dingley Dell
and grandfather's cottage grew white and strange.
It was as if every pine tree were a brown pole
we did not know; as if day had rearranged
into night and bats flew in sun. It was a trick
to turn around once and know you were lost;
knowing the crow's horn was crying in the dark,
knowing that supper would never come, that the coast's
cry of doom from that far away bell buoy's bell
said your nursemaid is gone
. O Mademoiselle,
the rowboat rocked over. Then you were dead.
Turn around once, eyes tight, the thought in your head.
Kind Sir: Lost and of your same kind
I have turned around twice with my eyes sealed
and the woods were white and my night mind
saw such strange happenings, untold and unreal.
And opening my eyes, I am afraid of course
to look-this inward look that society scorns-
Still, I search these woods and find nothing worse
than myself, caught between the grapes
and the thorns.

Knee Song

Being kissed on the back
of the knee is a moth
at the windowscreen and
yes my darling a dot
on the fathometer is
tinkerbelle with her cough
and twice I will give up my
honor and stars will stick
like tacks in the night
yes oh yes yes yes two
little snails at the back
of the knee building bonfires
something like eyelashes
something two zippos
striking yes yes yes small
and me maker.

Lament

Someone is dead.
Even the trees know it,
those poor old dancers who come on lewdly,
all pea-green scarfs and spine pole.
I think…
I think I could have stopped it,
if I'd been as firm as a nurse
or noticed the neck of the driver
as he cheated the crosstown lights;
or later in the evening,
if I'd held my napkin over my mouth.
I think I could…
if I'd been different, or wise, or calm,
I think I could have charmed the table,
the stained dish or the hand of the dealer.
But it's done.
It's all used up.
There's no doubt about the trees
spreading their thin feet into the dry grass.
A Canada goose rides up,
spread out like a gray suede shirt,
honking his nose into the March wind.
In the entryway a cat breathes calmly
into her watery blue fur.
The supper dishes are over and the sun
unaccustomed to anything else
goes an the way down.

Lessons In Hunger

'Do you like me?'
I asked the blue blazer.
No answer.
Silence bounced out of his books.
Silence fell off his tongue
and sat between us
and clogged my throat.
It slaughtered my trust.
It tore cigarettes out of my mouth.
We exchanged blind words,
and I did not cry,
and I did not beg,
blackness lunged in my heart,
and something that had been good,
a sort of kindly oxygen,
turned into a gas oven.
Do you like me?
How absurd!
What's a question like that?
What's a silence like that?
And what am I hanging around for,
riddled with what his silence said?

Letter Written On A Ferry While Crossing Long Island

Sound
I am surprised to see
that the ocean is still going on.
Now I am going back
and I have ripped my hand
from your hand as I said I would
and I have made it this far
as I said I would
and I am on the top deck now
holding my wallet, my cigarettes
and my car keys
at 2 o'clock on a Tuesday
in August of 1960.
Dearest,
although everything has happened,
nothing has happened.
The sea is very old.
the sea is the face of Mary,
without miracles or rage
or unusual hope,
grown rough and wrinkled
with incurable age.
Still,
I have eyes,
These are my eyes:
the orange letters that spell
ORIENT on the life preserver
that hangs by my knees;
the cement lifeboat that wears
its dirty canvas coat;
the faded sign that sits on its shelf

saying KEEP OFF.
Oh, alright, I say,
I'll save myself.
Over my right shoulder
I see four arms
who sit like a bridge club,
their faces poked out
from under their habits,
as good as good babies who
have sunk into their carriages.
Without discrimination
the wind pulls the skirts
of their arms.
Almost undressed,
I see what remains:
that holy wrist,
that ankle,
that chain.
Oh God,
although I am very sad,
could you please
let these four nuns
loosen their leather boots
and their wooden chairs
to rise out
over this greasy deck,
out over this iron rail,
nodding their pink heads to one side,
flying four abreast
in the old-fashioned side stroke;
each mouth open and round,
breathing together
as fish do,
singing without sound.
Dearest,

see how my dark girls sally forth,
over the passing lighthouse of Plum Gut,
its shell as rusty
as a camp dish,
as fragile as a pagoda
on a stone;
out over the little lighthouse
that warns me of drowning winds
that rub over its blind bottom
and its blue cover;
winds that will take the toes
and the ears of the rider
or the lover.
There go my dark girls,
their dresses puff
in the leeward air.
Oh, they are lighter than flying dogs
or the breath of dolphins;
each mouth opens gratefully,
wider than a milk cup.
My dark girls sing for this.
They are going up.
See them rise
on black wings, drinking
the sky, without smiles
or hands
or shoes.
They call back to us
from the gauzy edge of paradise,
good news, good news.

Live

Live or die, but don't poison everything…
Well, death's been here
for a long time -
it has a hell of a lot
to do with hell
and suspicion of the eye
and the religious objects
and how I mourned them
when they were made obscene
by my dwarf-heart's doodle.
The chief ingredient
is mutilation.
And mud, day after day,
mud like a ritual,
and the baby on the platter,
cooked but still human,
cooked also with little maggots,
sewn onto it maybe by somebody's mother,
the damn bitch!
Even so,
I kept right on going on,
a sort of human statement,
lugging myself as if
I were a sawed-off body
in the trunk, the steamer trunk.
This became perjury of the soul.
It became an outright lie
and even though I dressed the body
it was still naked, still killed.
It was caught
in the first place at birth,

like a fish.
But I play it, dressed it up,
dressed it up like somebody's doll.
Is life something you play?
And all the time wanting to get rid of it?
And further, everyone yelling at you
to shut up. And no wonder!
People don't like to be told
that you're sick
and then be forced
to watch you come
down with the hammer.
Today life opened inside me like an egg
and there inside
after considerable digging
I found the answer.
What a bargain!
There was the sun,
her yolk moving feverishly,
tumbling her prize -
and you realize she does this daily!
I'd known she was a purifier
but I hadn't thought
she was solid,
hadn't known she was an answer.
God! It's a dream,
lovers sprouting in the yard
like celery stalks
and better,
a husband straight as a redwood,
two daughters, two sea urchings,
picking roses off my hackles.
If I'm on fire they dance around it
and cook marshmallows.
And if I'm ice

they simply skate on me
in little ballet costumes.
Here,
all along,
thinking I was a killer,
anointing myself daily
with my little poisons.
But no.

I'm an empress.
I wear an apron.
My typewriter writes.
It didn't break the way it warned.
Even crazy, I'm as nice
as a chocolate bar.
Even with the witches' gymnastics
they trust my incalculable city,
my corruptible bed.
O dearest three,
I make a soft reply.
The witch comes on
and you paint her pink.
I come with kisses in my hood
and the sun, the smart one,
rolling in my arms.
So I say Live
and turn my shadow three times round
to feed our puppies as they come,
the eight Dalmatians we didn't drown,
despite the warnings: The abort! The destroy!
Despite the pails of water that waited,
to drown them, to pull them down like stones,
they came, each one headfirst, blowing bubbles
the color of cataract-blue
and fumbling for the tiny tits.

Just last week, eight Dalmatians,
3/4 of a lb., lined up like cord wood
each
like a
birch tree.
I promise to love more if they come,
because in spite of cruelty
and the stuffed railroad cars for the ovens,
I am not what I expected. Not an Eichmann.
The poison just didn't take.
So I won't hang around in my hospital shift,
repeating The Black Mass and all of it.
I say Live, Live because of the sun,
the dream, the excitable gift.

Lobster

A shoe with legs,
a stone dropped from heaven,
he does his mournful work alone,
he is the old prospector for golf,
with secret dreams of God-heads and fish heads.
Until suddenly a cradle fastens round him
and his is trapped as the U.S.A. sleeps.
Somewhere far off a woman lights a cigarette;
somewhere far off a car goes over a bridge;
somewhere far off a bank is held up.
This is the world the lobster knows not of.
He is the old hunting dog of the sea
who in the morning will rise from it
and be undrowned
and they will take his perfect green body
and paint it red.

Locked Doors

For the angels who inhabit this town,
although their shape constantly changes,
each night we leave some cold potatoes
and a bowl of milk on the windowsill.
Usually they inhabit heaven where,
by the way, no tears are allowed.
They push the moon around like
a boiled yam.
The Milky Way is their hen
with her many children.
When it is night the cows lie down
but the moon, that big bull,
stands up.
However, there is a locked room up there
with an iron door that can't be opened.
It has all your bad dreams in it.
It is hell.
Some say the devil locks the door
from the inside.
Some say the angels lock it from the outside.
The people inside have no water
and are never allowed to touch.
They crack like macadam.
They are mute.
They do not cry help
except inside
where their hearts are covered with grubs.
I would like to unlock that door,
turn the rusty key
and hold each fallen one in my arms
but I cannot, I cannot.

I can only sit here on earth
at my place at the table.

Love Letter Written In A Burning Building

I am in a crate, the crate that was ours,
full of white shirts and salad greens,
the icebox knocking at our delectable knocks,
and I wore movies in my eyes,
and you wore eggs in your tunnel,
and we played sheets, sheets, sheets
all day, even in the bathtub like lunatics.
But today I set the bed afire
and smoke is filling the room,
it is getting hot enough for the walls to melt,
and the icebox, a gluey white tooth.
I have on a mask in order to write my last words,
and they are just for you, and I will place them
in the icebox saved for vodka and tomatoes,
and perhaps they will last.
The dog will not. Her spots will fall off.
The old letters will melt into a black bee.
The night gowns are already shredding
into paper, the yellow, the red, the purple.
The bed - well, the sheets have turned to gold -
hard, hard gold, and the mattress
is being kissed into a stone.
As for me, my dearest Foxxy,
my poems to you may or may not reach the icebox
and its hopeful eternity,
for isn't yours enough?
The one where you name
my name right out in P.R.?
If my toes weren't yielding to pitch
I'd tell the whole story -
not just the sheet story

but the belly-button story,
the pried-eyelid story,
the whiskey-sour-of-the-nipple story -
and shovel back our love where it belonged.
Despite my asbestos gloves,
the cough is filling me with black and a
red powder seeps through my veins,
our little crate goes down so publicly
and without meaning it, you see, meaning a solo act,
a cremation of the love,
but instead we seem to be going down right in the middle of a
Russian
street,
the flames making the sound of
the horse being beaten and beaten,
the whip is adoring its human triumph
while the flies wait, blow by blow,
straight from United Fruit, Inc.

Lullaby

It is a summer evening.
The yellow moths sag
against the locked screens
and the faded curtains
suck over the window sills
and from another building
a goat calls in his dreams.
This is the TV parlor
in the best ward at Bedlam.
The night nurse is passing
out the evening pills.
She walks on two erasers,
padding by us one by one.
My sleeping pill is white.
It is a splendid pearl;
it floats me out of myself,
my stung skin as alien
as a loose bolt of cloth.
I will ignore the bed.
I am linen on a shelf.
Let the others moan in secret;
let each lost butterfly
go home. Old woolen head,
take me like a yellow moth
while the goat calls hush-a-bye.

Menstruation At Forty

I was thinking of a son.
The womb is not a clock
nor a bell tolling,
but in the eleventh month of its life
I feel the November
of the body as well as of the calendar.
In two days it will be my birthday
and as always the earth is done with its harvest.
This time I hunt for death,
the night I lean toward,
the night I want.
Well then—
speak of it!
It was in the womb all along.
I was thinking of a son ...
You! The never acquired,
the never seeded or unfastened,
you of the genitals I feared,
the stalk and the puppy's breath.
Will I give you my eyes or his?
Will you be the David or the Susan?
(Those two names I picked and listened for.)
Can you be the man your fathers are—
the leg muscles from Michelangelo,
hands from Yugoslavia
somewhere the peasant, Slavic and determined,
somewhere the survivor bulging with life—
and could it still be possible,
all this with Susan's eyes?
All this without you—
two days gone in blood.

I myself will die without baptism,
a third daughter they didn't bother.
My death will come on my name day.
What's wrong with the name day?

It's only an angel of the sun.
Woman,
weaving a web over your own,
a thin and tangled poison.
Scorpio,
bad spider—
die!
My death from the wrists,
two name tags,
blood worn like a corsage
to bloom
one on the left and one on the right—
It's a warm room,
the place of the blood.
Leave the door open on its hinges!
Two days for your death
and two days until mine.
Love! That red disease—
year after year, David, you would make me wild!
David! Susan! David! David!
full and disheveled, hissing into the night,
never growing old,
waiting always for you on the porch ...
year after year,
my carrot, my cabbage,
I would have possessed you before all women,
calling your name,
calling you mine.

More Than Myself

Not that it was beautiful,
but that, in the end, there was
a certain sense of order there;
something worth learning
in that narrow diary of my mind,
in the commonplaces of the asylum
where the cracked mirror
or my own selfish death
outstared me . . .
I tapped my own head;
it was glass, an inverted bowl.
It's small thing
to rage inside your own bowl.
At first it was private.
Then it was more than myself.

Mother And Daughter

Linda, you are leaving
your old body now,
It lies flat, an old butterfly,
all arm, all leg, all wing,
loose as an old dress.
I reach out toward it but
my fingers turn to cankers
and I am motherwarm and used,
just as your childhood is used.
Question you about this
and you hold up pearls.
Question you about this
and you pass by armies.
Question you about this -
you with your big clock going,
its hands wider than jackstraws -
and you'll sew up a continent.
Now that you are eighteen
I give you my booty, my spoils,
my Mother & Co. and my ailments.
Question you about this
and you'll not know the answer -
the muzzle at the oxygen,
the tubes, the pathways,
the war and the war's vomit.
Keep on, keep on, keep on,
carrying keepsakes to the boys,
carrying powders to the boys,
carrying, my Linda, blood to
the bloodletter.
Linda, you are leaving

your old body now.
You've picked my pocket clean
and you've racked up all my
poker chips and left me empty
and, as the river between us
narrows, you do calisthenics,
that womanly leggy semaphore.
Question you about this
and you will sew me a shroud
and hold up Monday's broiler
and thumb out the chicken gut.
Question you about this
and you will see my death
drooling at these gray lips
while you, my burglar, will eat
fruit and pass the time of day.

Mr. Mine

Notice how he has numbered the blue veins
in my breast. Moreover there are ten freckles.
Now he goes left. Now he goes right.
He is building a city, a city of flesh.
He's an industrialist. He has starved in cellars
and, ladies and gentlemen, he's been broken by iron,
by the blood, by the metal, by the triumphant
iron of his mother's death. But he begins again.
Now he constructs me. He is consumed by the city.
>From the glory of words he has built me up.
>From the wonder of concrete he has molded me.
He has given me six hundred street signs.
The time I was dancing he built a museum.
He built ten blocks when I moved on the bed.
He constructed an overpass when I left.
I gave him flowers and he built an airport.
For traffic lights he handed at red and green
lollipops. Yet in my heart I am go children slow.

Music Swims Back To Me

Wait Mister. Which way is home?
They turned the light out
and the dark is moving in the corner.
There are no sign posts in this room,
four ladies, over eighty,
in diapers every one of them.
La la la, Oh music swims back to me
and I can feel the tune they played
the night they left me
in this private institution on a hill.
Imagine it. A radio playing
and everyone here was crazy.
I liked it and danced in a circle.
Music pours over the sense
and in a funny way
music sees more than I.
I mean it remembers better;
remembers the first night here.
It was the strangled cold of November;
even the stars were strapped in the sky
and that moon too bright
forking through the bars to stick me
with a singing in the head.
I have forgotten all the rest.
They lock me in this chair at eight a.m.
and there are no signs to tell the way,
just the radio beating to itself
and the song that remembers
more than I. Oh, la la la,
this music swims back to me.
The night I came I danced a circle

and was not afraid.
Mister?

My Friend, My Friend

Who will forgive me for the things I do?
With no special legend of God to refer to,
With my calm white pedigree, my yankee kin,
I think it would be better to be a Jew.
I forgive you for what you did not do.
I am impossibly quilty. Unlike you,
My Friend, I can not blame my origin
With no special legend or God to refer to.
They wear The Crucifix as they are meant to do.
Why do their little crosses trouble you?
The effigies that I have made are genuine,
(I think it would be better to be a Jew).
Watching my mother slowly die I knew
My first release. I wish some ancient bugaboo
Followed me. But my sin is always my sin.
With no special legend or God to refer to.
Who will forgive me for the things I do?
To have your reasonable hurt to belong to
Might ease my trouble like liquor or aspirin.
I think it would be better to be a Jew.
And if I lie, I lie because I love you,
Because I am bothered by the things I do,
Because your hurt invades my calm white skin:
With no special legend or God to refer to,
I think it would be better to be a Jew.

Noon Walk On The Asylum Lawn

The summer sun ray
shifts through a suspicious tree.
though I walk through the valley of the shadow
It sucks the air
and looks around for me.
The grass speaks.
I hear green chanting all day.
I will fear no evil, fear no evil
The blades extend
and reach my way.
The sky breaks.
It sags and breathes upon my face.
In the presence of mine enemies, mine enemies
The world is full of enemies.
There is no safe place.

Oh

It is snowing and death bugs me
as stubborn as insomnia.
The fierce bubbles of chalk,
the little white lesions
settle on the street outside.
It is snowing and the ninety
year old woman who was combing
out her long white wraith hair
is gone, embalmed even now,
even tonight her arms are smooth
muskets at her side and nothing
issues from her but her last word - 'Oh.' Surprised by death.
It is snowing. Paper spots
are falling from the punch.
Hello? Mrs. Death is here!
She suffers according to the digits
of my hate. I hear the filaments
of alabaster. I would lie down
with them and lift my madness
off like a wig. I would lie
outside in a room of wool
and let the snow cover me.
Paris white or flake white
or argentine, all in the washbasin
of my mouth, calling, 'Oh.'
I am empty. I am witless.
Death is here. There is no
other settlement. Snow!
See the mark, the pock, the pock!
Meanwhile you pour tea
with your handsome gentle hands.

Then you deliberately take your
forefinger and point it at my temple,
saying, 'You suicide bitch!
I'd like to take a corkscrew
and screw out all your brains
and you'd never be back ever.'

And I close my eyes over the steaming
tea and see God opening His teeth.
'Oh.' He says.
I see the child in me writing, 'Oh.'
Oh, my dear, not why.

Old

I'm afraid of needles.
I'm tired of rubber sheets and tubes.
I'm tired of faces that I don't know
and now I think that death is starting.
Death starts like a dream,
full of objects and my sister's laughter.
We are young and we are walking
and picking wild blueberries.
all the way to Damariscotta.
Oh Susan, she cried.
you've stained your new waist.
Sweet taste -
my mouth so full
and the sweet blue running out
all the way to Damariscotta.
What are you doing? Leave me alone!
Can't you see I'm dreaming?
In a dream you are never eighty.

Old Dwarf Heart

True. All too true. I have never been at home in
life. All my decay has taken place upon a child.
Henderson the Rain King, by Saul Bellow
When I lie down to love,
old dwarf heart shakes her head.
Like an imbecile she was bom old.,
Her eyes wobble as thirty-one thick folds
of skin open to glare at me on my flickering bed.
She knows the decay we're made of.
When hurt she is abrupt.
Now she is solid, like fat,
breathing in loops like a green hen
in the dust. But if I dream of loving, then
my dreams are of snarling strangers. She dreams that…
strange, strange, and corrupt.
Good God, the things she knows!
And worse, the sores she holds
in her hands, gathered in like a nest
from an abandoned field. At her best
she is all red muscle, humming in and out, cajoled
by time. Where I go, she goes.
Oh now I lay me down to love,
how awkwardly her arms undo,
bow patiently I untangle her wrists
like knots. Old ornament, old naked fist,
even if I put on seventy coats I could not
cover you…
mother, father, I'm made of.

Portrait Of An Old Woman On The College Tavern Wall

Oh down at the tavern
the children are singing
around their round table
and around me still.
Did you hear what it said?
I only said
how there is a pewter urn
pinned to the tavern wall,
as old as old is able
to be and be there still.
I said, the poets are tere
I hear them singing and lying
around their round table
and around me still.
Across the room is a wreath
made of a corpse's hair,
framed in glass on the wall,
as old as old is able
to be and be remembered still.
Did you hear what it said?
I only said
how I want to be there and I
would sing my songs with the liars
and my lies with all the singers.
And I would, and I would but
it's my hair in the hair wreath,
my cup pinned to the tavern wall,
my dusty face they sing beneath.
Poets are sitting in my kitchen.
Why do these poets lie?
Why do children get children and
Did you hear what it said?
I only said
how I want to be there,

Oh, down at the tavern
where the prophets are singing
around their round table
until they are still.

Raccoon

Coon, why did you come to this dance
with a mask on? Why not the tin man
and his rainbow girl? Why not Racine,
his hair marcelled down to his chest?
Why not come as a stomach digesting
its worms? Why you little fellow
with your ears at attention and your
nose poking up like a microphone?
You whig emblem, you woman chaser,
who do you dance over the wide lawn tonight
clanging the garbage pail like great silver bells?

Rapunzel

A woman
who loves a woman
is forever young.
The mentor
and the student
feed off each other.
Many a girl
had an old aunt
who locked her in the study
to keep the boys away.
They would play rummy
or lie on the couch
and touch and touch.
Old breast against young breast…
Let your dress fall down your shoulder,
come touch a copy of you
for I am at the mercy of rain,
for I have left the three Christs of Ypsilanti
for I have left the long naps of Ann Arbor
and the church spires have turned to stumps.
The sea bangs into my cloister
for the politicians are dying,
and dying so hold me, my young dear,
hold me…
The yellow rose will turn to cinder
and New York City will fall in
before we are done so hold me,
my young dear, hold me.
Put your pale arms around my neck.
Let me hold your heart like a flower
lest it bloom and collapse.

Give me your skin
as sheer as a cobweb,
let me open it up
and listen in and scoop out the dark.
Give me your nether lips
all puffy with their art
and I will give you angel fire in return.
We are two clouds
glistening in the bottle glass.
We are two birds
washing in the same mirror.
We were fair game
but we have kept out of the cesspool.
We are strong.
We are the good ones.
Do not discover us
for we lie together all in green
like pond weeds.
Hold me, my young dear, hold me.
They touch their delicate watches
one at a time.
They dance to the lute
two at a time.
They are as tender as bog moss.
They play mother-me-do
all day.
A woman
who loves a woman
is forever young.
Once there was a witch's garden
more beautiful than Eve's
with carrots growing like little fish,
with many tomatoes rich as frogs,
onions as ingrown as hearts,
the squash singing like a dolphin

and one patch given over wholly to magic -
rampion, a kind of salad root
a kind of harebell more potent than penicillin,
growing leaf by leaf, skin by skin.
as rapt and as fluid as Isadoran Duncan.
However the witch's garden was kept locked
and each day a woman who was with child
looked upon the rampion wildly,
fancying that she would die
if she could not have it.
Her husband feared for her welfare
and thus climbed into the garden
to fetch the life-giving tubers.
Ah ha, cried the witch,
whose proper name was Mother Gothel,
you are a thief and now you will die.
However they made a trade,
typical enough in those times.
He promised his child to Mother Gothel
so of course when it was born
she took the child away with her.
She gave the child the name Rapunzel,
another name for the life-giving rampion.
Because Rapunzel was a beautiful girl
Mother Gothel treasured her beyond all things.
As she grew older Mother Gothel thought:
None but I will ever see her or touch her.
She locked her in a tow without a door
or a staircase. It had only a high window.
When the witch wanted to enter she cried'
Rapunzel, Rapunzel, let down your hair.
Rapunzel's hair fell to the ground like a rainbow.
It was as strong as a dandelion
and as strong as a dog leash.
Hand over hand she shinnied up

the hair like a sailor
and there in the stone-cold room,
as cold as a museum,
Mother Gothel cried:
Hold me, my young dear, hold me,
and thus they played mother-me-do.
Years later a prince came by
and heard Rapunzel singing her loneliness.
That song pierced his heart like a valentine
but he could find no way to get to her.
Like a chameleon he hid himself among the trees
and watched the witch ascend the swinging hair.
The next day he himself called out:
Rapunzel, Rapunzel, let down your hair,
and thus they met and he declared his love.
What is this beast, she thought,
with muscles on his arms
like a bag of snakes?
What is this moss on his legs?
What prickly plant grows on his cheeks?
What is this voice as deep as a dog?
Yet he dazzled her with his answers.
Yet he dazzled her with his dancing stick.
They lay together upon the yellowy threads,
swimming through them
like minnows through kelp
and they sang out benedictions like the Pope.
Each day he brought her a skein of silk
to fashion a ladder so they could both escape.
But Mother Gothel discovered the plot
and cut off Rapunzel's hair to her ears
and took her into the forest to repent.
When the prince came the witch fastened
the hair to a hook and let it down.
When he saw Rapunzel had been banished

he flung himself out of the tower, a side of beef.
He was blinded by thorns that prickled him like tacks.
As blind as Oedipus he wandered for years
until he heard a song that pierced his heart
like that long-ago valentine.
As he kissed Rapunzel her tears fell on his eyes
and in the manner of such cure-alls
his sight was suddenly restored.
They lived happily as you might expect
proving that mother-me-do
can be outgrown,
just as the fish on Friday,
just as a tricycle.
The world, some say,
is made up of couples.
A rose must have a stem.
As for Mother Gothel,
her heart shrank to the size of a pin,
never again to say: Hold me, my young dear,
hold me,
and only as she dreamed of the yellow hair
did moonlight sift into her mouth.

Red Riding Hood

Many are the deceivers:
The suburban matron,
proper in the supermarket,
list in hand so she won't suddenly fly,
buying her Duz and Chuck Wagon dog food,
meanwhile ascending from earth,
letting her stomach fill up with helium,
letting her arms go loose as kite tails,
getting ready to meet her lover
a mile down Apple Crest Road
in the Congregational Church parking lot.
Two seemingly respectable women
come up to an old Jenny
and show her an envelope
full of money
and promise to share the booty
if she'll give them ten thou
as an act of faith.
Her life savings are under the mattress
covered with rust stains
and counting.
They are as wrinkled as prunes
but negotiable.
The two women take the money and disappear.
Where is the moral?
Not all knives are for
stabbing the exposed belly.
Rock climbs on rock
and it only makes a seashore.
Old Jenny has lost her belief in mattresses
and now she has no wastebasket in which

to keep her youth.
The standup comic
on the 'Tonight' show
who imitates the Vice President
and cracks up Johnny Carson
and delays sleep for millions
of bedfellows watching between their feet,
slits his wrist the next morning
in the Algonquin's old-fashioned bathroom,
the razor in his hand like a toothbrush,
wall as anonymous as a urinal,
the shower curtain his slack rubberman audience,
and then the slash
as simple as opening as a letter
and the warm blood breaking out like a rose
upon the bathtub with its claw and ball feet.
And I. I too.
Quite collected at cocktail parties,
meanwhile in my head
I'm undergoing open-heart surgery.
The heart, poor fellow,
pounding on his little tin drum
with a faint death beat,
The heart, that eyeless beetle,
running panicked through his maze,
never stopping one foot after the other
one hour after the other
until he gags on an apple
and it's all over.
And I. I too again.
I built a summer house on Cape Ann.
A simple A-frame and this too was
a deception - nothing haunts a new house.
When I moved in with a bathing suit and tea bags
the ocean rumbled like a train backing up

and at each window secrets came in
like gas. My mother, that departed soul,
sat in my Eames chair and reproached me
for losing her keys to the old cottage.
Even in the electric kitchen there was
the smell of a journey. The ocean
was seeping through its frontiers
and laying me out on its wet rails.
The bed was stale with my childhood
and I could not move to another city
where the worthy make a new life.
Long ago
there was a strange deception:
a wolf dressed in frills,
a kind of transvestite.

But I get ahead of my story.
In the beginning
there was just little Red Riding Hood,
so called because her grandmother
made her a red cape and she was never without it.
It was her Linus blanket, besides
it was red, as red as the Swiss flag,
yes it was red, as red as chicken blood,
But more than she loved her riding hood
she loved her grandmother who lived
far from the city in the big wood.
This one day her mother gave her
a basket of wine and cake
to take to her grandmother
because she was ill.
Wine and cake?
Where's the aspirin? The penicillin?
Where's the fruit juice?
Peter Rabbit got chamomile tea.

But wine and cake it was.
On her way in the big wood
Red Riding Hood met the wolf.
Good day, Mr. Wolf, she said,
thinking him no more dangerous
than a streetcar or a panhandler.
He asked where she was going
and she obligingly told him
There among the roots and trunks
with the mushrooms pulsing inside the moss
he planned how to eat them both,
the grandmother an old carrot
and the child a shy budkin
in a red red hood.
He bade her to look at the bloodroot,
the small bunchberry and the dogtooth
and pick some for her grandmother.
And this she did.
Meanwhile he scampered off
to Grandmother's house and ate her up
as quick as a slap.
Then he put on her nightdress and cap
and snuggled down in to bed.

A deceptive fellow.
Red Riding hood
knocked on the door and entered
with her flowers, her cake, her wine.
Grandmother looked strange,
a dark and hairy disease it seemed.
Oh Grandmother, what big ears you have,
ears, eyes, hands and then the teeth.
The better to eat you with my dear.
So the wolf gobbled Red Riding Hood down
like a gumdrop. Now he was fat.

He appeared to be in his ninth month
and Red Riding Hood and her grandmother
rode like two Jonahs up and down with
his every breath. One pigeon. One partridge.
He was fast asleep,
dreaming in his cap and gown,
wolfless.
Along came a huntsman who heard
the loud contented snores
and knew that was no grandmother.
He opened the door and said,
So it's you, old sinner.
He raised his gun to shoot him
when it occurred to him that maybe
the wolf had eaten up the old lady.
So he took a knife and began cutting open
the sleeping wolf, a kind of caesarian section.
It was a carnal knife that let
Red Riding Hood out like a poppy,
quite alive from the kingdom of the belly.
And grandmother too
still waiting for cakes and wine.
The wolf, they decided, was too mean
to be simply shot so they filled his belly
with large stones and sewed him up.
He was as heavy as a cemetery
and when he woke up and tried to run off
he fell over dead. Killed by his own weight.
Many a deception ends on such a note.
The huntsman and the grandmother and
Red Riding Hood
sat down by his corpse and had
a meal of wine and cake.

Those two remembering

nothing naked and brutal
from that little death,
that little birth,
from their going down
and their lifting up.

Red Roses

Tommy is three and when he's bad
his mother dances with him.
She puts on the record,
'Red Roses for a Blue Lady'
and throws him across the room.
Mind you,
she never laid a hand on him.
He gets red roses in different places,
the head, that time he was as sleepy as a river,
the back, that time he was a broken scarecrow,
the arm like a diamond had bitten it,
the leg, twisted like a licorice stick,
all the dance they did together,
Blue Lady and Tommy.
You fell, she said, just remember you fell.
I fell, is all he told the doctors
in the big hospital. A nice lady came
and asked him questions but because
he didn't want to be sent away he said, I fell.
He never said anything else although he could talk fine.
He never told about the music
or how she'd sing and shout
holding him up and throwing him.
He pretends he is her ball.
He tries to fold up and bounce
but he squashes like fruit.
For he loves Blue Lady and the spots
of red roses he gives her

Ringing The Bells

And this is the way they ring
the bells in Bedlam
and this is the bell-lady
who comes each Tuesday morning
to give us a music lesson
and because the attendants make you go
and because we mind by instinct,
like bees caught in the wrong hive,
we are the circle of crazy ladies
who sit in the lounge of the mental house
and smile at the smiling woman
who passes us each a bell,
who points at my hand
that holds my bell, E flat,
and this is the gray dress next to me
who grumbles as if it were special
to be old, to be old,
and this is the small hunched squirrel girl
on the other side of me
who picks at the hairs over her lip,
who picks at the hairs over her lip all day,
and this is how the bells really sound,
as untroubled and clean
as a workable kitchen,
and this is always my bell responding
to my hand that responds to the lady
who points at me, E flat;
and although we are not better for it,
they tell you to go. And you do.

Rowing

A story, a story!
(Let it go. Let it come.)
I was stamped out like a Plymouth fender
into this world.
First came the crib
with its glacial bars.
Then dolls
and the devotion to their plactic mouths.
Then there was school,
the little straight rows of chairs,
blotting my name over and over,
but undersea all the time,
a stranger whose elbows wouldn't work.
Then there was life
with its cruel houses
and people who seldom touchedthough
touch is allbut
I grew,
like a pig in a trenchcoat I grew,
and then there were many strange apparitions,
the nagging rain, the sun turning into poison
and all of that, saws working through my heart,
but I grew, I grew,
and God was there like an island I had not rowed to,
still ignorant of Him, my arms, and my legs worked,
and I grew, I grew,
I wore rubies and bought tomatoes
and now, in my middle age,
about nineteen in the head I'd say,
I am rowing, I am rowing
though the oarlocks stick and are rusty
and the sea blinks and rolls
like a worried eyebal,

but I am rowing, I am rowing,
though the wind pushes me back
and I know that that island will not be perfect,
it will have the flaws of life,
the absurdities of the dinner table,
but there will be a door
and I will open it
and I will get rid of the rat insdie me,
the gnawing pestilential rat.
God will take it with his two hands
and embrace it.
As the African says:
This is my tale which I have told,
if it be sweet, if it be not sweet,
take somewhere else and let some return to me.
This story ends with me still rowing.

Rumpelstiltskin

Inside many of us
is a small old man
who wants to get out.
No bigger than a two-year-old
whom you'd call lamb chop
yet this one is old and malformed.
His head is okay
but the rest of him wasn't Sanforized?
He is a monster of despair.
He is all decay.
He speaks up as tiny as an earphone
with Truman's asexual voice:
I am your dwarf.
I am the enemy within.
I am the boss of your dreams.
No. I am not the law in your mind,
the grandfather of watchfulness.
I am the law of your members,
the kindred of blackness and impulse.
See. Your hand shakes.
It is not palsy or booze.
It is your Doppelganger
trying to get out.
Beware . . . Beware . . .
There once was a miller
with a daughter as lovely as a grape.
He told the king that she could
spin gold out of common straw.
The king summoned the girl
and locked her in a room full of straw
and told her to spin it into gold

or she would die like a criminal.
Poor grape with no one to pick.
Luscious and round and sleek.
Poor thing.
To die and never see Brooklyn.
She wept,
of course, huge aquamarine tears.
The door opened and in popped a dwarf.
He was as ugly as a wart.
Little thing, what are you? she cried.
With his tiny no-sex voice he replied:
I am a dwarf.
I have been exhibited on Bond Street
and no child will ever call me Papa.
I have no private life.
If I'm in my cups the whole town knows by breakfast
and no child will ever call me Papa
I am eighteen inches high.
I am no bigger than a partridge.
I am your evil eye
and no child will ever call me Papa.
Stop this Papa foolishness,
she cried. Can you perhaps
spin straw into gold?
Yes indeed, he said,
that I can do.
He spun the straw into gold
and she gave him her necklace
as a small reward.
When the king saw what she had done
he put her in a bigger room of straw
and threatened death once more.
Again she cried.
Again the dwarf came.
Again he spun the straw into gold.

She gave him her ring
as a small reward.
The king put her in an even bigger room
but this time he promised
to marry her if she succeeded.
Again she cried.
Again the dwarf came.
But she had nothing to give him.
Without a reward the dwarf would not spin.
He was on the scent of something bigger.
He was a regular bird dog.
Give me your first-born
and I will spin.
She thought: Piffle!
He is a silly little man.
And so she agreed.
So he did the trick.
Gold as good as Fort Knox.
The king married her
and within a year
a son was born.
He was like most new babies,
as ugly as an artichoke
but the queen thought him in pearl.
She gave him her dumb lactation,
delicate, trembling, hidden,
warm, etc.
And then the dwarf appeared
to claim his prize.
Indeed! I have become a papa!
cried the little man.
She offered him all the kingdom
but he wanted only this -
a living thing
to call his own.

And being mortal
who can blame him?
The queen cried two pails of sea water.
She was as persistent
as a Jehovah's Witness.
And the dwarf took pity.
He said: I will give you
three days to guess my name
and if you cannot do it
I will collect your child.
The queen sent messengers
throughout the land to find names
of the most unusual sort.
When he appeared the next day
she asked: Melchior?
Balthazar?
But each time the dwarf replied:
No! No! That's not my name.
The next day she asked:

Spindleshanks? Spiderlegs?
But it was still no-no.
On the third day the messenger
came back with a strange story.
He told her:
As I came around the corner of the wood
where the fox says good night to the hare
I saw a little house with a fire
burning in front of it.
Around that fire a ridiculous little man
was leaping on one leg and singing:
Today I bake.
Tomorrow I brew my beer.
The next day the queen's only child will be mine.
Not even the census taker knows

that Rumpelstiltskin is my name . . .
The queen was delighted.
She had the name!
Her breath blew bubbles.
When the dwarf returned
she called out:
Is your name by any chance Rumpelstiltskin?
He cried: The devil told you that!
He stamped his right foot into the ground
and sank in up to his waist.
Then he tore himself in two.
Somewhat like a split broiler.
He laid his two sides down on the floor,
one part soft as a woman,
one part a barbed hook,
one part papa,
one part Doppelganger.

Said The Poet To The Analyst

My business is words. Words are like labels,
or coins, or better, like swarming bees.
I confess I am only broken by the sources of things;
as if words were counted like dead bees in the attic,
unbuckled from their yellow eyes and their dry wings.
I must always forget how one word is able to pick
out another, to manner another, until I have got
something I might have said…
but did not.
Your business is watching my words. But I
admit nothing. I work with my best, for instance,
when I can write my praise for a nickel machine,
that one night in Nevada: telling how the magic jackpot
came clacking three bells out, over the lucky screen.
But if you should say this is something it is not,
then I grow weak, remembering how my hands felt funny
and ridiculous and crowded with all
the believing money.

Small Wire

My faith
is a great weight
hung on a small wire,
as doth the spider
hang her baby on a thin web,
as doth the vine,
twiggy and wooden,
hold up grapes
like eyeballs,
as many angels
dance on the head of a pin.
God does not need
too much wire to keep Him there,
just a thin vein,
with blood pushing back and forth in it,
and some love.
As it has been said:
Love and a cough
cannot be concealed.
Even a small cough.
Even a small love.
So if you have only a thin wire,
God does not mind.
He will enter your hands
as easily as ten cents used to
bring forth a Coke.

Snow White And The Seven Dwarfs

No matter what life you lead
the virgin is a lovely number:
cheeks as fragile as cigarette paper,
arms and legs made of Limoges,
lips like Vin Du Rhône,
rolling her china-blue doll eyes
open and shut.
Open to say,
Good Day Mama,
and shut for the thrust
of the unicorn.
She is unsoiled.
She is as white as a bonefish.
Once there was a lovely virgin
called Snow White.
Say she was thirteen.
Her stepmother,
a beauty in her own right,
though eaten, of course, by age,
would hear of no beauty surpassing her own.
Beauty is a simple passion,
but, oh my friends, in the end
you will dance the fire dance in iron shoes.
The stepmother had a mirror to which she referredsomething
like the weather forecasta
mirror that proclaimed
the one beauty of the land.
She would ask,
Looking glass upon the wall,
who is fairest of us all?
And the mirror would reply,
You are the fairest of us all.

Pride pumped in her like poison.
Suddenly one day the mirror replied,
Queen, you are full fair, 'tis true,
but Snow White is fairer than you.
Until that moment Snow White
had been no more important
than a dust mouse under the bed.
But now the queen saw brown spots on her hand
and four whiskers over her lip
so she condemned Snow White
to be hacked to death.
Bring me her heart, she said to the hunter,
and I will salt it and eat it.
The hunter, however, let his prisoner go
and brought a boar's heart back to the castle.
The queen chewed it up like a cube steak.
Now I am fairest, she said,
lapping her slim white fingers.
Snow White walked in the wildwood
for weeks and weeks.
At each turn there were twenty doorways
and at each stood a hungry wolf,
his tongue lolling out like a worm.
The birds called out lewdly,
talking like pink parrots,
and the snakes hung down in loops,
each a noose for her sweet white neck.
On the seventh week
she came to the seventh mountain
and there she found the dwarf house.
It was as droll as a honeymoon cottage
and completely equipped with
seven beds, seven chairs, seven forks
and seven chamber pots.
Snow White ate seven chicken livers

and lay down, at last, to sleep.
The dwarfs, those little hot dogs,
walked three times around Snow White,
the sleeping virgin. They were wise
and wattled like small czars.
Yes. It's a good omen,
they said, and will bring us luck.
They stood on tiptoes to watch
Snow White wake up. She told them
about the mirror and the killer-queen
and they asked her to stay and keep house.
Beware of your stepmother,
they said.
Soon she will know you are here.
While we are away in the mines
during the day, you must not
open the door.
Looking glass upon the wall...
The mirror told
and so the queen dressed herself in rags
and went out like a peddler to trap Snow White.
She went across seven mountains.
She came to the dwarf house
and Snow White opened the door
and bought a bit of lacing.
The queen fastened it tightly
around her bodice,
as tight as an Ace bandage,
so tight that Snow White swooned.
She lay on the floor, a plucked daisy.
When the dwarfs came home they undid the lace
and she revived miraculously.
She was as full of life as soda pop.
Beware of your stepmother,
they said.

She will try once more.
Looking glass upon the wall...
Once more the mirror told
and once more the queen dressed in rags
and once more Snow White opened the door.
This time she bought a poison comb,
a curved eight-inch scorpion,
and put it in her hair and swooned again.
The dwarfs returned and took out the comb
and she revived miraculously.
She opened her eyes as wide as Orphan Annie.
Beware, beware, they said,
but the mirror told,
the queen came,
Snow White, the dumb bunny,
opened the door
and she bit into a poison apple
and fell down for the final time.
When the dwarfs returned
they undid her bodice,
they looked for a comb,
but it did no good.
Though they washed her with wine
and rubbed her with butter
it was to no avail.
She lay as still as a gold piece.
The seven dwarfs could not bring themselves
to bury her in the black ground
so they made a glass coffin
and set it upon the seventh mountain
so that all who passed by
could peek in upon her beauty.
A prince came one June day
and would not budge.
He stayed so long his hair turned green

and still he would not leave.
The dwarfs took pity upon him
and gave him the glass Snow Whiteits
doll's eyes shut foreverto
keep in his far-off castle.
As the prince's men carried the coffin
they stumbled and dropped it
and the chunk of apple flew out
of her throat and she woke up miraculously.
And thus Snow White became the prince's bride.
The wicked queen was invited to the wedding feast
and when she arrived there were
red-hot iron shoes,
in the manner of red-hot roller skates,
clamped upon her feet.
First your toes will smoke
and then your heels will turn black
and you will fry upward like a frog,
she was told.
And so she danced until she was dead,
a subterranean figure,
her tongue flicking in and out
like a gas jet.
Meanwhile Snow White held court,
rolling her china-blue doll eyes open and shut
and sometimes referring to her mirror
as women do.

Some Foreign Letters

I knew you forever and you were always old,
soft white lady of my heart. Surely you would scold
me for sitting up late, reading your letters,
as if these foreign postmarks were meant for me.
You posted them first in London, wearing furs
and a new dress in the winter of eighteen-ninety.
I read how London is dull on Lord Mayor's Day,
where you guided past groups of robbers, the sad holes
of Whitechapel, clutching your pocketbook, on the way
to Jack the Ripper dissecting his famous bones.
This Wednesday in Berlin, you say, you will
go to a bazaar at Bismarck's house. And I
see you as a young girl in a good world still,
writing three generations before mine. I try
to reach into your page and breathe it back...
but life is a trick, life is a kitten in a sack.
This is the sack of time your death vacates.
How distant your are on your nickel-plated skates
in the skating park in Berlin, gliding past
me with your Count, while a military band
plays a Strauss waltz. I loved you last,
a pleated old lady with a crooked hand.
Once you read Lohengrin and every goose
hung high while you practiced castle life
in Hanover. Tonight your letters reduce
history to a guess. The count had a wife.
You were the old maid aunt who lived with us.
Tonight I read how the winter howled around
the towers of Schloss Schwobber, how the tedious
language grew in your jaw, how you loved the sound
of the music of the rats tapping on the stone
floors. When you were mine you wore an earphone.

This is Wednesday, May 9th, near Lucerne,
Switzerland, sixty-nine years ago. I learn
your first climb up Mount San Salvatore;
this is the rocky path, the hole in your shoes,
the yankee girl, the iron interior
of her sweet body. You let the Count choose
your next climb. You went together, armed
with alpine stocks, with ham sandwiches
and seltzer wasser. You were not alarmed
by the thick woods of briars and bushes,
nor the rugged cliff, nor the first vertigo
up over Lake Lucerne. The Count sweated
with his coat off as you waded through top snow.
He held your hand and kissed you. You rattled
down on the train to catch a steam boat for home;
or other postmarks: Paris, verona, Rome.
This is Italy. You learn its mother tongue.
I read how you walked on the Palatine among
the ruins of the palace of the Caesars;
alone in the Roman autumn, alone since July.
When you were mine they wrapped you out of here
with your best hat over your face. I cried
because I was seventeen. I am older now.
I read how your student ticket admitted you
into the private chapel of the Vatican and how
you cheered with the others, as we used to do
on the fourth of July. One Wednesday in November
you watched a balloon, painted like a silver abll,
float up over the Forum, up over the lost emperors,
to shiver its little modern cage in an occasional
breeze. You worked your New England
conscience out
beside artisans, chestnut vendors and the devout.
Tonight I will learn to love you twice;
learn your first days, your mid-Victorian face.

Tonight I will speak up and interrupt
your letters, warning you that wars are coming,
that the Count will die, that you will accept
your America back to live like a prim thing
on the farm in Maine. I tell you, you will come
here, to the suburbs of Boston, to see the blue-nose
world go drunk each night, to see the handsome
children jitterbug, to feel your left ear close
one Friday at Symphony. And I tell you,
you will tip your boot feet out of that hall,
rocking from its sour sound, out onto
the crowded street, letting your spectacles fall
and your hair net tangle as you stop passers-by
to mumble your guilty love while your ears die.

Song For A Lady

On the day of breasts and small hips
the window pocked with bad rain,
rain coming on like a minister,
we coupled, so sane and insane.
We lay like spoons while the sinister
rain dropped like flies on our lips
and our glad eyes and our small hips.
"The room is so cold with rain," you said
and you, feminine you, with your flower
said novenas to my ankles and elbows.
You are a national product and power.
Oh my swan, my drudge, my dear wooly rose,
even a notary would notarize our bed
as you knead me and I rise like bread.

Star-Nosed Mole

Mole, angel-dog of the pit,
digging six miles a night,
what's up with you in your sooty suit,
where's your kitchen at?
I find you at the edge of our pond,
drowned, numb drainer of weeds,
insects floating in your belly,
grubs like little fetuses bobbing
and your dear face with its fifth hand,
doesn't it know it's the end of the war?
It's all over, no need to go deep into ponds,
no fires, no cripples left.
Mole dog,
I wish your mother would wake you up
and you wouldn't lie there like the Pieta
wearing your cross on your nose.

Suicide Note

'You speak to me of narcissism but I reply that it is
a matter of my life' - Artaud
'At this time let me somehow bequeath all the leftovers
to my daughters and their daughters' - Anonymous
Better,
despite the worms talking to
the mare's hoof in the field;
better,
despite the season of young girls
dropping their blood;
better somehow
to drop myself quickly
into an old room.
Better (someone said)
not to be born
and far better
not to be born twice
at thirteen
where the boardinghouse,
each year a bedroom,
caught fire.
Dear friend,
I will have to sink with hundreds of others
on a dumbwaiter into hell.
I will be a light thing.
I will enter death
like someone's lost optical lens.
Life is half enlarged.
The fish and owls are fierce today.
Life tilts backward and forward.
Even the wasps cannot find my eyes.
Yes,

eyes that were immediate once.
Eyes that have been truly awake,
eyes that told the whole story—
poor dumb animals.
Eyes that were pierced,
little nail heads,
light blue gunshots.
And once with
a mouth like a cup,
clay colored or blood colored,
open like the breakwater
for the lost ocean
and open like the noose
for the first head.
Once upon a time
my hunger was for Jesus.
O my hunger! My hunger!
Before he grew old
he rode calmly into Jerusalem
in search of death.
This time
I certainly
do not ask for understanding
and yet I hope everyone else
will turn their heads when an unrehearsed fish jumps
on the surface of Echo Lake;
when moonlight,
its bass note turned up loud,
hurts some building in Boston,
when the truly beautiful lie together.
I think of this, surely,
and would think of it far longer
if I were not… if I were not
at that old fire.
I could admit

that I am only a coward
crying me me me
and not mention the little gnats, the moths,
forced by circumstance
to suck on the electric bulb.
But surely you know that everyone has a death,
his own death,
waiting for him.
So I will go now
without old age or disease,
wildly but accurately,
knowing my best route,
carried by that toy donkey I rode all these years,
never asking, "Where are we going?"
We were riding (if I'd only known)
to this.
Dear friend,
please do not think
that I visualize guitars playing
or my father arching his bone.
I do not even expect my mother's mouth.
I know that I have died before—
once in November, once in June.
How strange to choose June again,
so concrete with its green breasts and bellies.
Of course guitars will not play!
The snakes will certainly not notice.
New York City will not mind.
At night the bats will beat on the trees,
knowing it all,
seeing what they sensed all day.

Sylvia's Death

For Sylvia Plath
O Sylvia, Sylvia,
with a dead box of stones and spoons,

with two children, two meteors
wandering loose in a tiny playroom,

with your mouth into the sheet,
into the roofbeam, into the dumb prayer,

(Sylvia, Sylvia
where did you go
after you wrote me
from Devonshire
about raising potatoes
and keeping bees?)

what did you stand by,
just how did you lie down into?

Thief -
how did you crawl into,
crawl down alone
into the death I wanted so badly and for so long,

the death we said we both outgrew,
the one we wore on our skinny breasts,
the one we talked of so often each time
we downed three extra dry martinis in Boston,

the death that talked of analysts and cures,
the death that talked like brides with plots,
the death we drank to,
the motives and the quiet deed?

(In Boston
the dying
ride in cabs,
yes death again,
that ride home

with our boy.)
O Sylvia, I remember the sleepy drummer
who beat on our eyes with an old story,
how we wanted to let him come
like a sadist or a New York fairy
to do his job,
a necessity, a window in a wall or a crib,
and since that time he waited
under our heart, our cupboard,
and I see now that we store him up
year after year, old suicides
and I know at the news of your death
a terrible taste for it, like salt,
(And me,
me too.
And now, Sylvia,
you again
with death again,
that ride home
with our boy.)
And I say only
with my arms stretched out into that stone place,
what is your death
but an old belonging,
a mole that fell out
of one of your poems?
(O friend,
while the moon's bad,
and the king's gone,
and the queen's at her wit's end
the bar fly ought to sing!)
O tiny mother,
you too!
O funny duchess!
O blonde thing!

That Day

This is the desk I sit at
and this is the desk where I love you too much
and this is the typewriter that sits before me
where yesterday only your body sat before me
with its shoulders gathered in like a Greek chorus,
with its tongue like a king making up rules as he goes,
with its tongue quite openly like a cat lapping milk,
with its tongue - both of us coiled in its slippery life.
That was yesterday, that day.
That was the day of your tongue,
your tongue that came from your lips,
two openers, half animals, half birds
caught in the doorway of your heart.
That was the day I followed the king's rules,
passing by your red veins and your blue veins,
my hands down the backbone, down quick like a firepole,
hands between legs where you display your inner knowledge,
where diamond mines are buried and come forth to bury,
come forth more sudden than some reconstructed city.
It is complete within seconds, that monument.
The blood runs underground yet brings forth a tower.
A multitude should gather for such an edifice.
For a miracle one stands in line and throws confetti.
Surely The Press is here looking for headlines.
Surely someone should carry a banner on the sidewalk.
If a bridge is constructed doesn't
the mayor cut a ribbon?
If a phenomenon arrives shouldn't the
Magi come bearing gifts?
Yesterday was the day I bore gifts for your gift
and came from the valley to meet you on the pavement.

That was yesterday, that day.
That was the day of your face,
your face after love, close to the pillow, a lullaby.
Half asleep beside me letting the old fashioned rocker stop,
our breath became one, became a child-breath together,
while my fingers drew little o's on your shut eyes,
while my fingers drew little smiles on your mouth,
while I drew I LOVE YOU on your chest and its drummer
and whispered, 'Wake up!' and you mumbled in your sleep,
'Sh. We're driving to Cape Cod. We're heading for the Bourne

Bridge. We're circling the Bourne Circle.' Bourne!
Then I knew you in your dream and prayed of our time
that I would be pierced and you would take root in me
and that I might bring forth your born, might bear
the you or the ghost of you in my little household.
Yesterday I did not want to be borrowed
but this is the typewriter that sits before me
and love is where yesterday is at.

The Abortion

Somebody who should have been born
is gone.
Just as the earth puckered its mouth,
each bud puffing out from its knot,
I changed my shoes, and then drove south.
Up past the Blue Mountains, where
Pennsylvania humps on endlessly,
wearing, like a crayoned cat, its green hair,
its roads sunken in like a gray washboard;
where, in truth, the ground cracks evilly,
a dark socket from which the coal has poured,
Somebody who should have been born
is gone.
the grass as bristly and stout as chives,
and me wondering when the ground would break,
and me wondering how anything fragile survives;
up in Pennsylvania, I met a little man,
not Rumpelstiltskin, at all, at all…
he took the fullness that love began.
Returning north, even the sky grew thin
like a high window looking nowhere.
The road was as flat as a sheet of tin.
Somebody who should have been born
is gone.
Yes, woman, such logic will lead
to loss without death. Or say what you meant,
you coward…this baby that I bleed.

The Addict

Sleepmonger,
deathmonger,
with capsules in my palms each night,
eight at a time from sweet pharmaceutical bottles
I make arrangements for a pint-sized journey.
I'm the queen of this condition.
I'm an expert on making the trip
and now they say I'm an addict.
Now they ask why.
WHY!
Don't they know that I promised to die!
I'm keping in practice.
I'm merely staying in shape.
The pills are a mother, but better,
every color and as good as sour balls.
I'm on a diet from death.
Yes, I admit
it has gotten to be a bit of a habitblows
eight at a time, socked in the eye,
hauled away by the pink, the orange,
the green and the white goodnights.
I'm becoming something of a chemical
mixture.
that's it!
My supply
of tablets
has got to last for years and years.
I like them more than I like me.
It's a kind of marriage.
It's a kind of war where I plant bombs inside
of myself.

Yes
I try
to kill myself in small amounts,
an innocuous occupatin.

Actually I'm hung up on it.
But remember I don't make too much noise.
And frankly no one has to lug me out
and I don't stand there in my winding sheet.
I'm a little buttercup in my yellow nightie
eating my eight loaves in a row
and in a certain order as in
the laying on of hands
or the black sacrament.
It's a ceremony
but like any other sport
it's full of rules.
It's like a musical tennis match where
my mouth keeps catching the ball.
Then I lie on; my altar
elevated by the eight chemical kisses.
What a lay me down this is
with two pink, two orange,
two green, two white goodnights.
Fee-fi-fo-fum-
Now I'm borrowed.
Now I'm numb.

The Ambition Bird

So it has come to this
insomnia at 3:15 A.M.,
the clock tolling its engine
like a frog following
a sundial yet having an electric
seizure at the quarter hour.
The business of words keeps me awake.
I am drinking cocoa,
that warm brown mama.
I would like a simple life
yet all night I am laying
poems away in a long box.
It is my immortality box,
my lay-away plan,
my coffin.
All night dark wings
flopping in my heart.
Each an ambition bird.
The bird wants to be dropped
from a high place like Tallahatchie Bridge.
He wants to light a kitchen match
and immolate himself.
He wants to fly into the hand of Michelangelo
anc dome out painted on a ceiling.
He wants to pierce the hornet's nest
and come out with a long godhead.
He wants to take bread and wine
and bring forth a man happily floating in
the Caribbean.
He wants to be pressed out like a key
so he can unlock the Magi.
He wants to take leave among strangers

passing out bits of his heart like hors d'oeuvres.
He wants to die changing his clothes
and bolt for the sun like a diamond.
He wants, I want.
Dear God, wouldn't it be
good enough to just drink cocoa?
I must get a new bird
and a new immortality box.
There is folly enough inside this one.

The Angel Food Dogs

Leaping, leaping, leaping,
down line by line,
growling at the cadavers,
filling the holy jugs with their piss,
falling into windows and mauling the parents,
but soft, kiss-soft,
and sobbing sobbing
into their awful dog dish.
No point? No twist for you
in my white tunnel?
Let me speak plainly,
let me whisper it from the podium-
Mother, may I use your pseudonym?
May I take the dove named Mary
and shove out Anne?
May I take my check book, my holographs,
my eight naked books,
and sign it Mary, Mary, Mary
full of grace?
I know my name is not offensive
but my feet hang in the noose.
I want to be white.
I want to be blue.
I want to be a bee digging into an onion heart,
as you did to me, dug and squatted
long after death and its fang.
Hail Mary, full of me,
Nibbling in the sitting room of my head.
Mary, Mary, virgin forever,
whore forever,
give me your name,

give me your mirror.
Boils fester in my soul,
so give me your name so I may kiss them,
and they will fly off,
nameless
but named,
and they will fly off like angel food dogs
with thee
and with thy spirit.
Let me climb the face of my kitchen dog
and fly off into my terrified years.

The Assassin

The correct death is written in.
I will fill the need.
My bow is stiff.
My bow is in readiness.
I am the bullet and the hook.
I am cocked and held ready.
In my sights I carve him
like a sculptor. I mold out
his last look at everyone.
I carry his eyes and his
brain bone at every position.
I know his male sex and I do
march over him with my index finger.
His mouth and his anus are one.
I am at the center of feeling.
A subway train is
traveling across my crossbow.
I have a blood bolt
and I have made it mine.
With this man I take in hand
his destiny and with this gun
I take in hand the newspapers and
with my heat I will take him.
he will bend down toward me
and his veins will tumble out
like children… Give me
his flag and his eye.
Give me his hard shell and his lip.
He is my evil and my apple and
I will see him home.

The Author Of The Jesus Papers Speaks

In my dream
I milked a cow,
the terrible udder
like a great rubber lily
sweated in my fingers
and as I yanked,
waiting for the moon juice,
waiting for the white mother,
blood spurted from it
and covered me with shame.
Then God spoke to me and said:
People say only good things about Christmas.
If they want to say something bad,
they whisper.
So I went to the well and drew a baby
out of the hollow water.
Then God spoke to me and said:
Here. Take this gingerbread lady
and put her in your oven.
When the cow gives blood
and the Christ is born
we must all eat sacrifices.
We must all eat beautiful women.

The Balance Wheel

Where I waved at the sky
And waited your love through a February sleep,
I saw birds swinging in, watched them multiply
Into a tree, weaving on a branch, cradling a keep
In the arms of April sprung from the south to occupy
This slow lap of land, like cogs of some balance wheel.
I saw them build the air, with that motion birds feel.
Where I wave at the sky
And understand love, knowing our August heat,
I see birds pulling past the dim frosted thigh
Of Autumn, unlatched from the nest, and wing-beat
For the south, making their high dots across the sky,
Like beauty spots marking a still perfect cheek.
I see them bend the air, slipping away, for what birds seek.

The Ballad Of The Lonely Masturbator

The end of the affair is always death.
She's my workshop. Slippery eye,
out of the tribe of myself my breath
finds you gone. I horrify
those who stand by. I am fed.
At night, alone, I marry the bed.

Finger to finger, now she's mine.
She's not too far. She's my encounter.
I beat her like a bell. I recline
in the bower where you used to mount her.
You borrowed me on the flowered spread.
At night, alone, I marry the bed.

Take for instance this night, my love,
that every single couple puts together
with a joint overturning, beneath, above,
the abundant two on sponge and feather,
kneeling and pushing, head to head.
At night, alone, I marry the bed.

I break out of my body this way,
an annoying miracle. Could I
put the dream market on display?
I am spread out. I crucify.
My little plum is what you said.
At night, alone, I marry the bed.

Then my black-eyed rival came.
The lady of water, rising on the beach,
a piano at her fingertips, shame
on her lips and a flute's speech.
And I was the knock-kneed broom instead.
At night, alone, I marry the bed.

She took you the way a women takes

a bargain dress off the rack
and I broke the way a stone breaks.
I give back your books and fishing tack.
Today's paper says that you are wed.
At night, alone, I marry the bed.
The boys and girls are one tonight.
They unbutton blouses. They unzip flies.
They take off shoes. They turn off the light.

The glimmering creatures are full of lies.
They are eating each other. They are overfed.
At night, alone, I marry the bed.

The Bells

Today the circus poster
is scabbing off the concrete wall
and the children have forgotten
if they knew at all.
Father, do you remember?
Only the sound remains,
the distant thump of the good elephants,
the voice of the ancient lions
and how the bells
trembled for the flying man.
I, laughing,
lifted to your high shoulder
or small at the rough legs of strangers,
was not afraid.
You held my hand
and were instant to explain
the three rings of danger.
Oh see the naughty clown
and the wild parade
while love love
love grew rings around me.
this was the sound where it began;
our breath pounding up to see
the flying man breast out
across the boarded sky
and climb the air.
I remember the color of music
and how forever
all the trembling bells of you
were mine.

The Big Boots Of Pain

There can be certain potions
needled in the clock
for the body's fall from grace,
to untorture and to plead for.
These I have known
and would sell all my furniture
and books and assorted goods
to avoid, and more, more.
But the other pain
I would sell my life to avoid
the pain that begins in the crib
with its bars or perhaps
with your first breath
when the planets drill
your future into you
for better of worse
as you marry life
and the love that gets doled out
or doesn't.
I find now, swallowing one teaspoon
of pain, that it drops downward
to the past where it mixes
with last year's cupful
and downward into a decade's quart
and downward into a lifetime's ocean.
I alternate treading water
and deadman's float.
The teaspoon ought to be hearable
if it didn't mix into the reruns
and thus enlarge into what it is not,

a sea pest's sting turning promptly
into the shark's neat biting off
of a leg because the soul
wears a magnifying glass.
Kicking the heart
with pain's big boots running up and down
the intestines like a motorcycle racer.
Yet one does get out of bed
and start over, plunge into the day
and put on a hopeful look
and does not allow fear to build a wall
between you and an old friend
or a new friend and reach out your hand,
shutting down the thought that
an axe may cut it off unexpectedly.
One learns not to blab about all this
except to yourself or the typewriter keys
who tell no one until they get brave
and crawl off onto the printed page.
I'm getting bored with it,
I tell the typewriter,
this constantly walking around
in wet shoes and then, surprise!
Somehow DECEASED keeps getting
stamped in red over the word HOPE.
And I who keep falling thankfully
into each new pillow of belief,
finding my Mercy Street,
kissing it and tenderly gift-wrapping my love,
am beginning to wonder just what
the planets had in mind on November 9th, 1928.
The pillows are ripped away,
the hand guillotined,
dog shit thrown into the middle of a laugh,
a hornets' nest building into the hi-fi speaker

and leaving me in silence,
where, without music,
I become a cracked orphan.
Well,
one gets out of bed
and the planets don't always hiss
or muck up the day, each day.
As for the pain and its multiplying teaspoon,
perhaps it is a medicine
that will cure the soul
of its greed for love
next Thursday.

The Big Heart

'Too many things are occurring for even a big heart to hold.' - From
an essay by
W. B. Yeats
Big heart,
wide as a watermelon,
but wise as birth,
there is so much abundance
in the people I have:
Max, Lois, Joe, Louise,
Joan, Marie, Dawn,
Arlene, Father Dunne,
and all in their short lives
give to me repeatedly,
in the way the sea
places its many fingers on the shore,
again and again
and they know me,
they help me unravel,
they listen with ears made of conch shells,
they speak back with the wine of the best region.
They are my staff.
They comfort me.
They hear how
the artery of my soul has been severed
and soul is spurting out upon them,
bleeding on them,
messing up their clothes,
dirtying their shoes.
And God is filling me,
though there are times of doubt

as hollow as the Grand Canyon,
still God is filling me.
He is giving me the thoughts of dogs,
the spider in its intricate web,
the sun
in all its amazement,
and a slain ram
that is the glory,
the mystery of great cost,
and my heart,
which is very big,
I promise it is very large,
a monster of sorts,
takes it all in—
all in comes the fury of love.

The Black Art

A woman who writes feels too much,
those trances and portents!
As if cycles and children and islands
weren't enough; as if mourners and gossips
and vegetables were never enough.
She thinks she can warn the stars.
A writer is essentially a spy.
Dear love, I am that girl.
A man who writes knows too much,
such spells and fetiches!
As if erections and congresses and products
weren't enough; as if machines and galleons
and wars were never enough.
With used furniture he makes a tree.
A writer is essentially a crook.
Dear love, you are that man.
Never loving ourselves,
hating even our shoes and our hats,
we love each other, precious, precious.
Our hands are light blue and gentle.
Our eyes are full of terrible confessions.
But when we marry,
the children leave in disgust.
There is too much food and no one left over
to eat up all the weird abundance.

The Break

It was also my violent heart that broke,
falling down the front hall stairs.
It was also a message I never spoke,
calling, riser after riser, who cares
about you, who cares, splintering up
the hip that was merely made of crystal,
the post of it and also the cup.
I exploded in the hallway like a pistol.
So I fell apart. So I came all undone.
Yes. I was like a box of dog bones.
But now they've wrapped me in like a nun.
Burst like firecrackers! Held like stones!
What a feat sailing queerly like Icarus
until the tempest undid me and I broke.
The ambulance drivers made such a fuss.
But when I cried, 'Wait for my courage!' they smoked
and then they placed me, tied me up on their plate,
and wheeled me out to their coffin, my nest.
Slowly the siren slowly the hearse, sedate
as a dowager. At the E. W. they cut off my dress.
I cried, 'Oh Jesus, help me! Oh Jesus Christ!'
and the nurse replied, 'Wrong name. My name
is Barbara,' and hung me in an odd device,
a buck's extension and a Balkan overhead frame.
The orthopedic man declared,
'You'll be down for a year.' His scoop. His news.
He opened the skin. He scraped. He pared
and drilled through bone for his four-inch screws.
That takes brute strength like pushing a cow
up hill. I tell you, it takes skill

and bedside charm and all that know how.
The body is a damn hard thing to kill.

But please don't touch or jiggle my bed.
I'm Ethan Frome's wife. I'll move when I'm able.
The T. V. hangs from the wall like a moose head.
I hide a pint of bourbon in my bedside table.
A bird full of bones, now I'm held by a sand bag.
The fracture was twice. The fracture was double.
The days are horizontal. The days are a drag.
All of the skeleton in me is in trouble.
Across the hall is the bedpan station.
The urine and stools pass hourly by my head
in silver bowls. They flush in unison
in the autoclave. My one dozen roses are dead.
The have ceased to menstruate. They hang
there like little dried up blood clots.
And the heart too, that cripple, how it sang
once. How it thought it could call the shots!
Understand what happened the day I fell.
My heart had stammered and hungered at
a marriage feast until the angel of hell
turned me into the punisher, the acrobat.
My bones are loose as clothespins,
as abandoned as dolls in a toy shop
and my heart, old hunger motor, with its sins
revved up like an engine that would not stop.
And now I spend all day taking care
of my body, that baby. Its cargo is scarred.
I anoint the bedpan. I brush my hair,
waiting in the pain machine for my bones to get hard,
for the soft, soft bones that were laid apart
and were screwed together. They will knit.
And the other corpse, the fractured heart,
I feed it piecemeal, little chalice. I'm good to it.

Yet lie a fire alarm it waits to be known.

It is wired. In it many colors are stored.
While my body's in prison, heart cells alone
have multiplied. My bones are merely bored
with all this waiting around. But the heart,
this child of myself that resides in the flesh,
this ultimate signature of the me, the start
of my blindness and sleep, builds a death crèche.
The figures are placed at the grave of my bones.
All figures knowing it is the other death
they came for. Each figure standing alone.
The heart burst with love and lost its breath.
This little town, this little country is real
and thus it is so of the post and the cup
and thus of the violent heart. The zeal
of my house doth eat me up.

The Break Away

Your daisies have come
on the day of my divorce:
the courtroom a cement box,
a gas chamber for the infectious Jew in me
and a perhaps land, a possibly promised land
for the Jew in me,
but still a betrayal room for the till-death-do-us—
and yet a death, as in the unlocking of scissors
that makes the now separate parts useless,
even to cut each other up as we did yearly
under the crayoned-in sun.
The courtroom keeps squashing our lives as they break
into two cans ready for recycling,
flattened tin humans
and a tin law,
even for my twenty-five years of hanging on
by my teeth as I once saw at Ringling Brothers.
The gray room:
Judge, lawyer, witness
and me and invisible Skeezix,
and all the other torn
enduring the bewilderments
of their division.
Your daisies have come
on the day of my divorce.
They arrive like round yellow fish,
sucking with love at the coral of our love.
Yet they wait,
in their short time,
like little utero half-borns,

half killed, thin and bone soft.
They breathe the air that stands
for twenty-five illicit days,
the sun crawling inside the sheets,
the moon spinning like a tornado
in the washbowl,
and we orchestrated them both,
calling ourselves TWO CAMP DIRECTORS.

There was a song, our song on your cassette,
that played over and over
and baptised the prodigals.
It spoke the unspeakable,
as the rain will on an attic roof,
letting the animal join its soul
as we kneeled before a miracleforgetting
its knife.
The daisies confer
in the old-married kitchen
papered with blue and green chefs
who call out pies, cookies, yummy,
at the charcoal and cigarette smoke
they wear like a yellowy salve.
The daisies absorb it allthe
twenty-five-year-old sanctioned love
(If one could call such handfuls of fists
and immobile arms that!)
and on this day my world rips itself up
while the country unfastens along
with its perjuring king and his court.
It unfastens into an abortion of belief,
as in methe
legal riftas
on might do with the daisies
but does not

for they stand for a love
undergoihng open heart surgery
that might take
if one prayed tough enough.
And yet I demand,
even in prayer,
that I am not a thief,
a mugger of need,
and that your heart survive
on its own,
belonging only to itself,
whole, entirely whole,
and workable
in its dark cavern under your ribs.

I pray it will know truth,
if truth catches in its cup
and yet I pray, as a child would,
that the surgery take.
I dream it is taking.
Next I dream the love is swallowing itsclf.
Next I dream the love is made of glass,
glass coming through the telephone
that is breaking slowly,
day by day, into my ear.
Next I dream that I put on the love
like a lifejacket and we float,
jacket and I,
we bounce on that priest-blue.
We are as light as a cat's ear
and it is safe,
safe far too long!
And I awaken quickly and go to the opposite window
and peer down at the moon in the pond
and know that beauty has walked over my head,

into this bedroom and out,
flowing out through the window screen,
dropping deep into the water
to hide.
I will observe the daisies
fade and dry up
wuntil they become flour,
snowing themselves onto the table
beside the drone of the refrigerator,
beside the radio playing Frankie
(as often as FM will allow)
snowing lightly, a tremor sinking from the ceilingas
twenty-five years split from my side
like a growth that I sliced off like a melanoma.
It is six P.M. as I water these tiny weeds
and their little half-life,
their numbered days
that raged like a secret radio,
recalling love that I picked up innocently,
yet guiltily,
as my five-year-old daughter
picked gum off the sidewalk
and it became suddenly an elastic miracle.
For me it was love found
like a diamond
where carrots growthe
glint of diamond on a plane wing,
meaning: DANGER! THICK ICE!
but the good crunch of that orange,
the diamond, the carrot,
both with four million years of resurrecting dirt,
and the love,
although Adam did not know the word,
the love of Adam
obeying his sudden gift.

You, who sought me for nine years,
in stories made up in front of your naked mirror
or walking through rooms of fog women,
you trying to forget the mother
who built guilt with the lumber of a locked door
as she sobbed her soured mild and fed you loss
through the keyhole,
you who wrote out your own birth
and built it with your own poems,
your own lumber, your own keyhole,
into the trunk and leaves of your manhood,
you, who fell into my words, years
before you fell into me (the other,
both the Camp Director and the camper),
you who baited your hook with wide-awake dreams,
and calls and letters and once a luncheon,
and twice a reading by me for you.
But I wouldn't!
Yet this year,
yanking off all past years,
I took the bait
and was pulled upward, upward,
into the sky and was held by the sunwww.
the quick wonder of its yellow lapand
became a woman who learned her own shin
and dug into her soul and found it full,
and you became a man who learned his won skin
and dug into his manhood, his humanhood
and found you were as real as a baker
or a seer
and we became a home,
up into the elbows of each other's soul,
without knowingan
invisible purchasethat
inhabits our house forever.

We were
blessed by the House-Die
by the altar of the color T.V.
and somehow managed to make a tiny marriage,
a tiny marriage
called belief,
as in the child's belief in the tooth fairy,
so close to absolute,
so daft within a year or two.
The daisies have come
for the last time.
And I who have,
each year of my life,
spoken to the tooth fairy,
believing in her,
even when I was her,
am helpless to stop your daisies from dying,
although your voice cries into the telephone:
Marry me! Marry me!
and my voice speaks onto these keys tonight:
The love is in dark trouble!
The love is starting to die,
right nowwe
are in the process of it.
The empty process of it.
I see two deaths,
and the two men plod toward the mortuary of my heart,
and though I willed one away in court today
and I whisper dreams and birthdays into the other,
they both die like waves breaking over me
and I am drowning a little,
but always swimming
among the pillows and stones of the breakwater.
And though your daisies are an unwanted death,
I wade through the smell of their cancer

and recognize the prognosis,
its cartful of loss-
I say now,
you gave what you could.
It was quite a ferris wheel to spin on!
and the dead city of my marriage
seems less important
than the fact that the daisies came weekly,
over and over,
likes kisses that can't stop themselves.
There sit two deaths on November 5th, 1973.
Let one be forgotten-
Bury it! Wall it up!
But let me not forget the man
of my child-like flowers
though he sinks into the fog of Lake Superior,
he remains, his fingers the marvel
of fourth of July sparklers,
his furious ice cream cones of licking,
remains to cool my forehead with a washcloth
when I sweat into the bathtub of his being.
For the rest that is left:
name it gentle,
as gentle as radishes inhabiting
their short life in the earth,
name it gentle,
gentle as old friends waving so long at the window,
or in the drive,
name it gentle as maple wings singing
themselves upon the pond outside,
as sensuous as the mother-yellow in the pond,
that night that it was ours,
when our bodies floated and bumped
in moon water and the cicadas
called out like tongues.

Let such as this
be resurrected in all men
whenever they mold their days and nights
as when for twenty-five days and nights you molded mine
and planted the seed that dives into my God
and will do so forever
no matter how often I sweep the floor.

The Breast

This is the key to it.
This is the key to everything.
Preciously.
I am worse than the gamekeeper's children
picking for dust and bread.
Here I am drumming up perfume.
Let me go down on your carpet,
your straw mattress - whatever's at hand
because the child in me is dying, dying.
It is not that I am cattle to be eaten.
It is not that I am some sort of street.
But your hands found me like an architect.
Jugful of milk! It was yours years ago
when I lived in the valley of my bones,
bones dumb in the swamp. Little playthings.
A xylophone maybe with skin
stretched over it awkwardly.
Only later did it become something real.
Later I measured my size against movie stars.
I didn't measure up. Something between
my shoulders was there. But never enough.
Sure, there was a meadow,
but no yound men singing the truth.
Nothing to tell truth by.
Ignorant of men I lay next to my sisters
and rising out of the ashes I cried
my sex will be transfixed!
Now I am your mother, your daughter,
your brand new thing - a snail, a nest.
I am alive when your fingers are.

I wear silk - the cover to uncover -
because silk is what I want you to think of.
But I dislike the cloth. It is too stern.
So tell me anything but track me like a climber
for here is the eye, here is the jewel,
here is the excitement the nipple learns.
I am unbalanced - but I am not mad with snow.
I am mad the way young girls are mad,
with an offering, an offering…
I burn the way money burns.

The Child Bearers

Jean, death comes close to us all,
flapping its awful wings at us
and the gluey wings crawl up our nose.
Our children tremble in their teen-age cribs,
whirling off on a thumb or a motorcycle,
mine pushed into gnawing a stilbestrol cancer
I passed on like hemophilia,
or yours in the seventh grade, with her spleen
smacked in by the balance beam.
And we, mothers, crumpled, and flyspotted
with bringing them this far
can do nothing now but pray.
Let us put your three children
and my two children,
ages ranging from eleven to twenty-one,
and send them in a large air net up to God,
with many stamps, real air mail,
and huge signs attached:
SPECIAL HANDLING.
DO NOT STAPLE, FOLD OR MUTILATE!
And perhaps He will notice
and pass a psalm over them
for keeping safe for a whole,
for a whole God-damned life-span.
And not even a muddled angel will
peek down at us in our foxhole.
And He will not have time
to send down an eyedropper of prayer for us,
the mothering thing of us,
as we drip into the soup

and drown
in the worry festering inside us,
lest our children
go so fast
they go.

The Children

The children are all crying in their pens
and the surf carries their cries away.
They are old men who have seen too much,
their mouths are full of dirty clothes,
the tongues poverty, tears like puss.
The surf pushes their cries back.
Listen.
They are bewitched.
They are writing down their life
on the wings of an elf
who then dissolves.
They are writing down their life
on a century fallen to ruin.
They are writing down their life
on the bomb of an alien God.
I am too.
We must get help.
The children are dying in their pens.
Their bodies are crumbling.
Their tongues are twisting backwards.
There is a certain ritual to it.
There is a dance they do in their pens.
Their mouths are immense.
They are swallowing monster hearts.
So is my mouth.
Listen.
We must all stop dying in the little ways,
in the craters of hate,
in the potholes of indifferencea
murder in the temple.

The place I live in
is a maze
and I keep seeking
the exit or the home.
Yet if I could listen
to the bulldog courage of those children
and turn inward into the plague of my soul
with more eyes than the stars
I could melt the darknessas
suddenly as that time
when an awful headache goes away
or someone puts out the fireand
stop the darkness and its amputations
and find the real McCoy
in the private holiness
of my hands.

The Civil War

I am torn in two
but I will conquer myself.
I will dig up the pride.
I will take scissors
and cut out the beggar.
I will take a crowbar
and pry out the broken
pieces of God in me.
Just like a jigsaw puzzle,
I will put Him together again
with the patience of a chess player.
How many pieces?
It feels like thousands,
God dressed up like a whore
in a slime of green algae.
God dressed up like an old man
staggering out of His shoes.
God dressed up like a child,
all naked,
even without skin,
soft as an avocado when you peel it.
And others, others, others.
But I will conquer them all
and build a whole nation of God
in me - but united,
build a new soul,
dress it with skin
and then put on my shirt
and sing an anthem,
a song of myself.

The Consecrating Mother

I stand before the sea
and it rolls and rolls in its green blood
saying, 'Do not give up one god
for I have a handful.'
The trade winds blew
in their twelve-fingered reversal
and I simply stood on the beach
while the ocean made a cross of salt
and hung up its drowned
and they cried Deo Deo.
The ocean offered them up in the vein of its might.
I wanted to share this
but I stood alone like a pink scarecrow.
The ocean steamed in and out,
the ocean gasped upon the shore
but I could not define her,
I could not name her mood, her locked-up faces.
Far off she rolled and rolled
like a woman in labor
and I thought of those who had crossed her,
in antiquity, in nautical trade, in slavery, in war.
I wondered how she had borne those bulwarks.
She should be entered skin to skin,
and put on like one's first or last cloth,
envered like kneeling your way into church,
descending into that ascension,
though she be slick as olive oil,
as she climbs each wave like an embezzler of white.
The big deep knows the law as it wears its gray hat,
though the ocean comes in its destiny,
with its one hundred lips,

and in moonlight she comes in her nudity,
flashing breasts made of milk-water,
flashing buttocks made of unkillable lust,
and at night when you enter her
you shine like a neon soprano.
I am that clumsy human
on the shore
loving you, coming, coming,
going,
and wish to put my thumb on you
like The Song of Solomon.

The Dead Heart

After I wrote this, a friend scrawled on this page, "Yes."
And I said, merely to myself, "I wish it could be for a
different seizure—as with Molly Bloom and her 'and
yes I said yes I will Yes.'
It is not a turtle
hiding in its little green shell.
It is not a stone
to pick up and put under your black wing.
It is not a subway car that is obsolete.
It is not a lump of coal that you could light.
It is a dead heart.
It is inside of me.
It is a stranger
yet once it was agreeable,
opening and closing like a clam.
What it has cost me you can't imagine,
shrinks, priests, lovers, children, husbands,
friends and all the lot.
An expensive thing it was to keep going.
It gave back too.
Don't deny it!
I half wonder if April would bring it back to life?
A tulip? The first bud?
But those are just musings on my part,
the pity one has when one looks at a cadaver.
How did it die?
I called it EVIL.
I said to it, your poems stink like vomit.
I didn't stay to hear the last sentence.
It died on the word EVIL.

It did it with my tongue.
The tongue, the Chinese say,
is like a sharp knife:
it kills
without drawing blood.

The Death Baby

1. DREAMS

I was an ice baby.
I turned to sky blue.
My tears became two glass beads.
My mouth stiffened into a dumb howl.
They say it was a dream
but I remember that hardening.
My sister at six
dreamt nightly of my death:
'The baby turned to ice.
Someone put her in the refrigerator
and she turned as hard as a Popsicle.'
I remember the stink of the liverwurst.
How I was put on a platter and laid
between the mayonnaise and the bacon.
The rhythm of the refrigerator
had been disturbed.
The milk bottle hissed like a snake.
The tomatoes vomited up their stomachs.
The caviar turned to lave.
The pimentos kissed like cupids.
I moved like a lobster,
slower and slower.
The air was tiny.
The air would not do.
*

I was at the dogs' party.
I was their bone.
I had been laid out in their kennel
like a fresh turkey.

This was my sister's dream
but I remember that quartering;
I remember the sickbed smell
of the sawdust floor, the pink eyes,
the pink tongues and the teeth, those nails.
I had been carried out like Moses
and hidden by the paws
of ten Boston bull terriers,
ten angry bulls
jumping like enormous roaches.
At first I was lapped,
rough as sandpaper.
I became very clean.
Then my arm was missing.
I was coming apart.
They loved me until
I was gone.
2. THE DY-DEE DOLL
My Dy-dee doll
died twice.
Once when I snapped
her head off
and let if float in the toilet
and once under the sun lamp
trying to get warm
she melted.
She was a gloom,
her face embracing
her little bent arms.
She died in all her rubber wisdom.
3. SEVEN TIMES
I died seven times
in seven ways
letting death give me a sign,
letting death place his mark on my forehead,

crossed over, crossed over
And death took root in that sleep.
In that sleep I held an ice baby
and I rocked it
and was rocked by it.
Oh Madonna, hold me.
I am a small handful.
NA
My mother died
unrocked, unrocked.
Weeks at her deathbed
seeing her thrust herself against the metal bars,
thrashing like a fish on the hook
and me low at her high stage,
letting the priestess dance alone,
wanting to place my head in her lap
or even take her in my arms somehow
and fondle her twisted gray hair.
But her rocking horse was pain
with vomit steaming from her mouth.
Her belly was big with another child,
cancer's baby, big as a football.
I could not soothe.
With every hump and crack
there was less Madonna
until that strange labor took her.
Then the room was bankrupt.
That was the end of her paying.
5. MAX
Max and I
two immoderate sisters,
two immoderate writers,
two burdeners,
made a pact.
To beat death down with a stick.

To take over.
To build our death like carpenters.
When she had a broken back,
each night we built her sleep.
Talking on the hot line
until her eyes pulled down like shades.
And we agreed in those long hushed phone calls
that when the moment comes
we'll talk turkey,
we'll shoot words straight from the hip,
we'll play it as it lays.
Yes,
when death comes with its hood
we won't be polite.

6. BABY

Death,
you lie in my arms like a cherub,
as heavy as bread dough.
Your milky wings are as still as plastic.
Hair soft as music.
Hair the color of a harp.
And eyes made of glass,
as brittle as crystal.
Each time I rock you
I think you will break.
I rock. I rock.
Glass eye, ice eye,
primordial eye,
lava eye,
pin eye,
break eye,
how you stare back!
Like the gaze if small children
you know all about me.
You have worn my underwear.

You have read my newspaper.
You have seen my father whip me.
You have seen my stroke my father's whip.
I rock. I rock.
We plunge back and forth
comforting each other.
We are stone.
We are carved, a pietà
that swings.
Outside, the world is a chilly army.
Outside, the sea is brought to its knees.
Outside, Pakistan is swallowed in a mouthful.
I rock. I rock.
You are my stone child
with still eyes like marbles.
There is a death baby
for each of us.
We own him.
His smell is our smell.
Beware. Beware.
There is a tenderness.
There is a love
for this dumb traveler
waiting in his pink covers.
Someday,
heavy with cancer or disaster
I will look up at Max
and say: It is time.
Hand me the death baby
and there will be
that final rocking.

The Death King

I hired a carpenter
to build my coffin
and last night I lay in it,
braced by a pillow,
sniffing the wood,
letting the old king
breathe on me,
thinking of my poor murdered body,
murdered by time,
waiting to turn stiff as a field marshal,
letting the silence dishonor me,
remembering that I'll never cough again.
Death will be the end of fear
and the fear of dying,
fear like a dog stuffed in my mouth,
feal like dung stuffed up my nose,
fear where water turns into steel,
fear as my breast flies into the Disposall,
fear as flies tremble in my ear,
fear as the sun ignites in my lap,
fear as night can't be shut off,
and the dawn, my habitual dawn,
is locked up forever.
Fear and a coffin to lie in
like a dead potato.
Even then I will dance in my dire clothes,
a crematory flight,
blinding my hair and my fingers,
wounding God with his blue face,
his tyranny, his absolute kingdom,
with my aphrodisiac.

The Division Of Parts

1.
Mother, my Mary Gray,
once resident of Gloucester
and Essex County,
a photostat of your will
arrived in the mail today.
This is the division of money.
I am one third
of your daughters counting my bounty
or I am a queen alone
in the parlor still,
eating the bread and honey.
It is Good Friday.
Black birds pick at my window sill.
Your coat in my closet,
your bright stones on my hand,
the gaudy fur animals
I do not know how to use,
settle on me like a debt.
A week ago, while the hard March gales
beat on your house,
we sorted your things: obstacles
of letters, family silver,
eyeglasses and shoes.
Like some unseasoned Christmas, its scales
rigged and reset,
I bundled out gifts I did not choose.
Now the houts of The Cross
rewind. In Boston, the devout
work their cold knees
toward that sweet martyrdom

that Christ planned. My timely loss
is too customary to note; and yet
I planned to suffer
and I cannot. It does not please
my yankee bones to watch
where the dying is done
in its usly hours. Black birds peck
at my window glass
and Easter will take its ragged son.
The clutter of worship
that you taught me, Mary Gray,
is old. I imitate
a memory of belief
that I do not own. I trip
on your death and jesus, my stranger
floats up over
my Christian home, wearing his straight
thorn tree. I have cast my lot
and am one third thief
of you. Time, that rearranger
of estates, equips
me with your garments, but not with grief.
2.
This winter when
cancer began its ugliness
I grieved with you each day
for three months
and found you in your private nook
of the medicinal palace
for New England Women
and never once
forgot how long it took.
I read to you
from The New Yorker, ate suppers
you wouldn't eat, fussed

with your flowers,
joked with your nurses, as if I
were the balm among lepers,
as if I could undo
a life in hours
if I never said goodbye.
But you turned old,
all your fifty-eight years sliding
like masks from your skull;
and at the end
I packed your nightgowns in suitcases,
paid the nurses, came riding
home as if I'd been told
I could pretend
people live in places.
3.
Since then I have pretended ease,
loved with the trickeries of need, but not enough
to shed my daughterhood
or sweeten him as a man.
I drink the five o' clock martinis
and poke at this dry page like a rough
goat. Fool! I fumble my lost childhood
for a mother and lounge in sad stuff
with love to catch and catch as catch can.
And Christ still waits. I have tried
to exorcise the memory of each event
and remain still, a mixed child,
heavy with cloths of you.
Sweet witch, you are my worried guide.
Such dangerous angels walk through Lent.
Their walls creak Anne! Convert! Convert!
My desk moves. Its cavr murmurs Boo
and I am taken and beguiled.
Or wrong. For all the way I've come

I'll have to go again. Instead, I must convert
to love as reasonable
as Latin, as sold as earthenware:
an equilibrium
I never knew. And Lent will keep its hurt
for someone else. Christ knows enough
staunch guys have hitched him in trouble.
thinking his sticks were badges to wear.
4.
Spring rusts on its skinny branch
and last summer's lawn
is soggy and brown.
Yesterday is just a number.
All of its winters avalanche
out of sight. What was, is gone.
Mother, last night I slept
in your Bonwit Teller nightgown.
Divided, you climbed into my head.
There in my jabbering dream
I heard my own angry cries
and I cursed you, Dame
keep out of my slumber.
My good Dame, you are dead.
And Mother, three stones
slipped from your glittering eyes.
Now it's Friday's noon
and I would still curse
you with my rhyming words
and bring you flapping back, old love,
old circus knitting, god-in-her-moon,
all fairest in my lang syne verse,
the gauzy bride among the children,
the fancy amid the absurd
and awkward, that horn for hounds
that skipper homeward, that museum

keeper of stiff starfish, that blaze
within the pilgrim woman,
a clown mender, a dove's
cheek among the stones,
my Lady of first words,
this is the division of ways.
And now, while Christ stays
fastened to his Crucifix
so that love may praise
his sacrifice
and not the grotesque metaphor,
you come, a brave ghost, to fix
in my mind without praise
or paradise
to make me your inheritor.

The Doctor Of The Heart

Take away your knowledge, Doktor.
It doesn't butter me up.
You say my heart is sick unto.
You ought to have more respect!
you with the goo on the suction cup.
You with your wires and electrodes
fastened at my ankle and wrist,
sucking up the biological breast.
You with your zigzag machine
playing like the stock market up and down.
Give me the Phi Beta key you always twirl
and I will make a gold crown for my molar.
I will take a slug if you please
and make myself a perfectly good appendix.
Give me a fingernail for an eyeglass.
The world was milky all along.
I will take an iron and press out
my slipped disk until it is flat.
But take away my mother's carcinoma
for I have only one cup of fetus tears.
Take away my father's cerebral hemorrhage
for I have only a jigger of blood in my hand.
Take away my sister's broken neck
for I have only my schoolroom ruler for a cure.
Is there such a device for my heart?
I have only a gimmick called magic fingers.

Let me dilate like a bad debt.
Here is a sponge. I can squeeze it myself.
O heart, tobacco red heart,

beat like a rock guitar.
I am at the ship's prow.
I am no longer the suicide
with her raft and paddle.
Herr Doktor! I'll no longer die
to spite you, you wallowing
seasick grounded man.

The Double Image

1.

I am thirty this November.
You are still small, in your fourth year.
We stand watching the yellow leaves go queer,
flapping in the winter rain.
falling flat and washed. And I remember
mostly the three autumns you did not live here.
They said I'd never get you back again.
I tell you what you'll never really know:
all the medical hypothesis
that explained my brain will never be as true as these
struck leaves letting go.
I, who chose two times
to kill myself, had said your nickname
the mewling mouths when you first came;
until a fever rattled
in your throat and I moved like a pantomine
above your head. Ugly angels spoke to me. The blame,
I heard them say, was mine. They tattled
like green witches in my head, letting doom
leak like a broken faucet;
as if doom had flooded my belly and filled your bassinet,
an old debt I must assume.
Death was simpler than I'd thought.
The day life made you well and whole
I let the witches take away my guilty soul.
I pretended I was dead
until the white men pumped the poison out,
putting me armless and washed through the rigamarole
of talking boxes and the electric bed.

I laughed to see the private iron in that hotel.
Today the yellow leaves
go queer. You ask me where they go I say today believed
in itself, or else it fell.
Today, my small child, Joyce,
love your self's self where it lives.
There is no special God to refer to; or if there is,
why did I let you grow
in another place. You did not know my voice
when I came back to call. All the superlatives
of tomorrow's white tree and mistletoe
will not help you know the holidays you had to miss.
The time I did not love
myself, I visited your shoveled walks; you held my glove.
There was new snow after this.
2.
They sent me letters with news
of you and I made moccasins that I would never use.
When I grew well enough to tolerate
myself, I lived with my mother, the witches said.
But I didn't leave. I had my portrait
done instead.
Part way back from Bedlam
I came to my mother's house in Gloucester,
Massachusetts. And this is how I came
to catch at her; and this is how I lost her.
I cannot forgive your suicide, my mother said.
And she never could. She had my portrait
done instead.
I lived like an angry guest,
like a partly mended thing, an outgrown child.
I remember my mother did her best.
She took me to Boston and had my hair restyled.
Your smile is like your mother's, the artist said.
I didn't seem to care. I had my portrait

done instead.
There was a church where I grew up
with its white cupboards where they locked us up,
row by row, like puritans or shipmates
singing together. My father passed the plate.
Too late to be forgiven now, the witches said.
I wasn't exactly forgiven. They had my portrait
done instead.

3.

All that summer sprinklers arched
over the seaside grass.
We talked of drought
while the salt-parched
field grew sweet again. To help time pass
I tried to mow the lawn
and in the morning I had my portrait done,
holding my smile in place, till it grew formal.
Once I mailed you a picture of a rabbit
and a postcard of Motif number one,
as if it were normal
to be a mother and be gone.
They hung my portrait in the chill
north light, matching
me to keep me well.
Only my mother grew ill.
She turned from me, as if death were catching,
as if death transferred,
as if my dying had eaten inside of her.
That August you were two, by
I timed my days with doubt.
On the first of September she looked at me
and said I gave her cancer.
They carved her sweet hills out
and still I couldn't answer.

4.

That winter she came
part way back
from her sterile suite
of doctors, the seasick
cruise of the X-ray,
the cells' arithmetic
gone wild. Surgery incomplete,
the fat arm, the prognosis poor, I heard
them say.

During the sea blizzards
she had here
own portrait painted.
A cave of mirror
placed on the south wall;
matching smile, matching contour.
And you resembled me; unacquainted
with my face, you wore it. But you were mine
after all.
I wintered in Boston,
childless bride,
nothing sweet to spare
with witches at my side.
I missed your babyhood,
tried a second suicide,
tried the sealed hotel a second year.
On April Fool you fooled me. We laughed and this
was good.
5.
I checked out for the last time
on the first of May;
graduate of the mental cases,
with my analysts's okay,
my complete book of rhymes,
my typewriter and my suitcases.

All that summer I learned life
back into my own
seven rooms, visited the swan boats,
the market, answered the phone,
served cocktails as a wife
should, made love among my petticoats
and August tan. And you came each
weekend. But I lie.
You seldom came. I just pretended
you, small piglet, butterfly
girl with jelly bean cheeks,
disobedient three, my splendid
stranger. And I had to learn
why I would rather
die than love, how your innocence
would hurt and how I gather
guilt like a young intern
his symptons, his certain evidence.
That October day we went
to Gloucester the red hills
reminded me of the dry red fur fox
coat I played in as a child; stock still
like a bear or a tent,
like a great cave laughing or a red fur fox.
We drove past the hatchery,
the hut that sells bait,
past Pigeon Cove, past the Yacht Club, past Squall's
Hill, to the house that waits
still, on the top of the sea,
and two portraits hung on the opposite walls.
6.
In north light, my smile is held in place,
the shadow marks my bone.
What could I have been dreaming as I sat there,
all of me waiting in the eyes, the zone

of the smile, the young face,
the foxes' snare.
In south light, her smile is held in place,
her cheeks wilting like a dry
orchid; my mocking mirror, my overthrown
love, my first image. She eyes me from that face
that stony head of death
I had outgrown.
The artist caught us at the turning;
we smiled in our canvas home
before we chose our foreknown separate ways.
The dry redfur fox coat was made for burning.

I rot on the wall, my own
Dorian Gray.
And this was the cave of the mirror,
that double woman who stares
at herself, as if she were petrified
in time - two ladies sitting in umber chairs.
You kissed your grandmother
and she cried.
7.
I could not get you back
except for weekends. You came
each time, clutching the picture of a rabbit
that I had sent you. For the last time I unpack
your things. We touch from habit.
The first visit you asked my name.
Now you will stay for good. I will forget
how we bumped away from each other
like marionettes
on strings. It wasn't the same
as love, letting weekends contain
us. You scrape your knee. You learn my name,
wobbling up the sidewalk, calling and crying.

You can call me mother and I remember my mother again,
somewhere in greater Boston, dying.
I remember we named you Joyce
so we could call you Joy.
You came like an awkward guest
that first time, all wrapped and moist
and strange at my heavy breast.
I needed you. I didn't want a boy,
only a girl, a small milky mouse
of a girl, already loved, already loud in the house
of herself. We named you Joy.
I, who was never quite sure
about being a girl, needed another
life, another image to remind me.
And this was my worst guilt; you could not cure
or soothe it. I made you to find me.

The Earth

God loafs around heaven,
without a shape
but He would like to smoke His cigar
or bite His fingernails
and so forth.
God owns heaven
but He craves the earth,
the earth with its little sleepy caves,
its bird resting at the kitchen window,
even its murders lined up like broken chairs,
even its writers digging into their souls
with jackhammers,
even its hucksters selling their animals
for gold,
even its babies sniffing for their music,
the farm house, white as a bone,
sitting in the lap of its corn,
even the statue holding up its widowed life,
but most of all He envies the bodies,
He who has no body.
The eyes, opening and shutting like keyholes
and never forgetting, recording by thousands,
the skull with its brains like eelsthe
tablet of the worldthe
bones and their joints
that build and break for any trick,
the genitals,
the ballast of the eternal,
and the heart, of course,
that swallows the tides

and spits them out cleansed.
He does not envy the soul so much.
He is all soul
but He would like to house it in a body
and come down
and give it a bath
now and then.

The Earth Falls Down

If I could blame it all on the weather,
the snow like the cadaver's table,
the trees turned into knitting needles,
the ground as hard as a frozen haddock,
the pond wearing its mustache of frost.
If I could blame conditions on that,
if I could blame the hearts of strangers
striding muffled down the street,
or blame the dogs, every color,
sniffing each other
and pissing on the doorstep…
If I could blame the bosses
and the presidents for
their unpardonable songs…
If I could blame it on all
the mothers and fathers of the world,
they of the lessons, the pellets of power,
they of the love surrounding you like batter…
Blame it on God perhaps?
He of the first opening
that pushed us all into our first mistakes?
No, I'll blame it on Man
For Man is God
and man is eating the earth up
like a candy bar
and not one of them can be left alone with the ocean
for it is known he will gulp it all down.
The stars (possibly) are safe.
At least for the moment.
The stars are pears

that no one can reach,
even for a wedding.
Perhaps for a death.

The Errand

I've been going right on, page by page,
since we last kissed, two long dolls in a cage,
two hunger-mongers throwing a myth in and out,
double-crossing out lives with doubt,
leaving us separate now, fogy with rage.
But then I've told my readers what I think
and scrubbed out the remainder with my shrink,
have placed my bones in a jar as if possessed,
have pasted a black wing over my left breast,
have washed the white out of the moon at my sink,
have eaten The Cross, have digested its lore,
indeed, have loved that eggless man once more,
have placed my own head in the kettle because
in the end death won't settle for my hypochondrias,
because this errand we're on goes to one store.
That shopkeeper may put up barricades,
and he may advertise cognac and razor blades,
he may let you dally at Nice or the Tuileries,
he may let the state of our bowels have ascendancy,
he may let such as we flaunt our escapades,
swallow down our portion of whisky and dex,
salvage the day with some soup or some sex,
juggle our teabags as we inch down the hall,
let the blood out of our fires with phenobarbital,
lick the headlines for Starkweathers and Specks,
let us be folk of the literary set,
let us deceive with words the critics regret,
let us dog down the streets for each invitation,
typing out our lives like a Singer sewing sublimation,
letting our delicate bottoms settle and yet

they were spanked alive by some doctor of folly,
given a horn or a dish to get by with, by golly,
exploding with blood in this errand called life,
dumb with snow and elbows, rubber man, a mother wife,
tongues to waggle out of the words, mistletoe and holly,
tables to place our stones on, decades of disguises,
wntil the shopkeeper plants his boot in our eyes,
and unties our bone and is finished with the case,
and turns to the next customer, forgetting our face
or how we knelt at the yellow bulb with sighs
like moth wings for a short while in a small place.

The Evil Eye

It comes oozing
out of flowers at night,
it comes out of the rain
if a snake looks skyward,
it comes out of chairs and tables
if you don't point at them and say their names.
It comes into your mouth while you sleep,
pressing in like a washcloth.
Beware. Beware.
If you meet a cross-eyed person
you must plunge into the grass,
alongside the chilly ants,
fish through the green fingernails
and come up with the four-leaf clover
or your blood with congeal
like cold gravy.
If you run across a horseshoe,
passerby,
stop, take your hands out of your pockets
and count the nails
as you count your children
or your money.
Otherwise a sand flea will crawl in your ear
and fly into your brain
and the only way you'll keep from going mad
is to be hit with a hammer every hour.
If a hunchback is in the elevator with you
don't turn away,
immediately touch his hump
for his child will be born from his back tomorrow

and if he promptly bites the baby's nails off
(so it won't become a thief)
that child will be holy
and you, simple bird that you are,
may go on flying.

When you knock on wood,
and you do,
you knock on the Cross
and Jesus gives you a fragment of His body
and breaks an egg in your toilet,
giving up one life
for one life.

The Evil Seekers

We are born with luck
which is to say with gold in our mouth.
As new and smooth as a grape,
as pure as a pond in Alaska,
as good as the stem of a green beanwe
are born and that ought to be enough,
we ought to be able to carry on from that
but one must learn about evil,
learn what is subhuman,
learn how the blood pops out like a scream,
one must see the night
before one can realize the day,
one must listen hard to the animal within,
one must walk like a sleepwalker
on the edge of a roof,
one must throw some part of her body
into the devil's mouth.
Odd stuff, you'd say.
But I'd say
you must die a little,
have a book of matches go off in your hand,
see your best friend copying your exam,
visit an Indian reservation and see
their plastic feathers,
the dead dream.
One must be a prisoner just once to hear
the lock twist into his gut.
After all that
one is free to grasp at the trees, the stones,
the sky, the birds that make sense out of air.

But even in a telephone booth
evil can seep out of the receiver
and we must cover it with a mattress,
and then tear it from its roots
and bury it,
bury it.

The Exorcists

And I solemnly swear
on the chill of secrecy
that I know you not, this room never,
the swollen dress I wear,
nor the anonymous spoons that free me,
nor this calendar nor the pulse we pare and cover.
For all these present,
before that wandering ghost,
that yellow moth of my summer bed,
I say: this small event
is not. So I prepare, am dosed
in ether and will not cry what stays unsaid.
I was brown with August,
the clapping waves at my thighs
and a storm riding into the cove. We swam
while the others beached and burst
for their boarded huts, their hale cries
shouting back to us and the hollow slam
of the dory against the float.
Black arms of thunder strapped
upon us, squalled out, we breathed in rain
and stroked past the boat.
We thrashed for shore as if we were trapped
in green and that suddenly inadequate stain
of lightning belling around
our skin. Bodies in air
we raced for the empty lobsterman-shack.
It was yellow inside, the sound
of the underwing of the sun. I swear,
I most solemnly swear, on all the bric-a-brac

of summer loves, I know
you not.

The Expatriates

My dear, it was a moment
to clutch for a moment
so that you may believe in it
and believing is the act of love, I think,
even in the telling, wherever it went.
In the false New England forest
where the misplanted Norwegian trees
refused to root, their thick synthetic
roots barging out of the dirt to work on the air,
we held hands and walked on our knees.
Actually, there was no one there.
For fourty years this experimental
woodland grew, shaft by shaft in perfect rows
where its stub branches held and its spokes fell.
It was a place of parallel trees, their lives
filed out in exile where we walked too alien to know
our sameness and how our sameness survives.
Outside of us the village cars followed
the white line we had carefully walked
two nights before toward our single beds.
We lay halfway up an ugly hill and if we fell
it was here in the woods where the woods were caught
in their dying and you held me well.
And now I must dream the forest whole
and your sweet hands, not once as frozen
as those stopped trees, nor ruled, nor pale,
nor leaving mine. Today in my house, I see
our house, its pillars a dim basement of men
holding up their foreign ground for you and me.
My dear, it was a time,

butchered from time
that we must tell of quickly
before we lose the sound of our own
mouths calling mine, mine, mine.

The Fallen Angels

They come on to my clean
sheet of paper and leave a Rorschach blot.
They do not do this to be mean,
they do it to give me a sign
they want me, as Aubrey Beardsley once said,
to shove it around till something comes.
Clumsy as I am,
I do it.
For I am like them -
both saved and lost,
tumbling downward like Humpty Dumpty
off the alphabet.
Each morning I push them off my bed
and when they get in the salad
rolling in it like a dog,
I pick each one out
just the way my daughter
picks out the anchovies.
In May they dance on the jonquils,
wearing out their toes,
laughing like fish.
In November, the dread month,
they suck the childhood out of the berries
and turn them sour and inedible.
Yet they keep me company.
They wiggle up life.
They pass out their magic
like Assorted Lifesavers.
They go with me to the dentist
and protect me form the drill.

At the same time,
they go to class with me
and lie to my students.
O fallen angel,
the companion within me,
whisper something holy
before you pinch me
into the grave.

www.ingramcontent.com/pod-product-compliance
Lightning Source LLC
Chambersburg PA
CBHW020905160726
47993CB00005B/1821